THE POETRY ORACLE

Written and Edited by:

Amber Guetebier
& Brenda Knight

CONSORTIUM OF COLLECTIVE CONSCIOUSNESS

www.cccpublishing.com   www.thepoetryoracle.com

The Poems
—OF—

The Poetry Oracle

first edition

Copyright © 2008

by Amber Guetebier & Brenda Knight

Published by the Consortium of Collective Consciousness ™

Requests for permission or further information should be addressed to CCC Publishing, 530 8th Avenue #6, San Francisco, CA 94118 USA. FAX (415) 933-8132.

Cover design by Elizabeth Jens

Library of Congress Control Number: 2008935293

Includes index (Pbk.)

ISBN-13: 978-1888729207

ISBN-10: 1888729201

1. Spirituality—Metaphysics, Oracle. 2. Poetry—Classics.
Printed in the United States of America.

10 9 8 7 6 5 4 3 2 1

Table of Contents

Introduction

Do you find the idea that you can connect with the divine powers of prophecy simply by opening this book a bit unsettling? Don't be alarmed, dear querent, it is a time-honored tradition handed down to us from the very ancients who first realized you could consult supernatural sources for knowledge of the future.

The legendary Oracle at Delphi was, to the ancient Greeks, a source of inspiration, prophecies, and divine messages from the Gods and Goddesses who ruled the heavens and reigned over the Earth. In ancient Greece, a rhapsody was an epic poem, or part of one, and as common for communicating stories and great tales of adventure as

The Poetry Oracle

today's daily news. Calliope, the Muse of epic poetry, and Polyhymnia, the Muse of sacred poetry were invoked to create stories of adventure, love, and death in a verse form, a story that would last throughout time.

So too, has modern poetry, evolved from this ancient tradition. Poets keep the sacred art alive and pay homage to the muses by expressing their truths and imagery in a way that defies time and place. It is with all of this in mind that we have created The Poetry Oracle, rekindling the ancient practice of rhapsodomancy; divination using verse or poetry. We invite you, dear reader, to find the answers to your wildest question, to seek guidance from The Poetry Oracle, to find a bit of poetry that will get you through the day. In keeping with the divine purpose that has inspired us to create The Poetry Oracle,

we have used bibliomancy to choose many of the quotes we offer you here, and have employed the "cut-up technique," made so famous by The Beats, to select the order of the quotes themselves.

As poets, we have written thousands of words, but as lovers of poetry we have read thousands more. Each one of these lines stands out in their own way, marking a passage of a moment, a memory, a sensation. Consult this Oracle, and re-visit poetry in a whole new way. Teach your children how to be poetry. Call upon the spirits of Sappho and Kerouac, of Plath and Dickenson, Keats and weiss. Ask these poets, in the name of Polyhymnia, to guide you to the words that will open your mind's eye to a literal world of metaphors. Consult The Poetry Oracle.

How to Use "The Poetry Oracle"

The Poetry Oracle is designed to be spontaneous, just like poetry itself. While there are no hard and fast rules to consulting The Poetry Oracle, we offer these guidelines to loosely follow. Are you a haiku person, or do you prefer free verse? Your own preference will guide you to the manner in which you use The Poetry Oracle.

Set the book upon a flat surface; if no surface is available, you may hold the book in your open palms.

For questions of a more serious nature, candle light is recommended, and it is even more divine if this is the only light in the room. Fire light is also nice. The Poetry Oracle is very personal. You decide what you will seek from it.

The Poetry Oracle

Close your eyes and concentrate on the question or quandary at hand. When you have taken the time to really focus on what you need to know, keeping your eyes closed, begin to flip the pages. Stop when you feel you have reached a place that will answer your imploring thoughts, and use your index finger to point to a place on the page. Open your eyes and read the passage nearest your finger. This is the gift that The Poetry Oracle offers you.

To remain truly inspired, you may want to use that verse to start a free-write of your own. Or perhaps if you are in a group, the stanzas all fit together somehow? The Poetry Oracle strives to pay tribute to the thousands of poignant words that have changed our thinking. We invite you to join along.

Love is the fire, and sighs the smoke,
The ashes, shame and scornes

Robert Southwell, "The Burning Babe"

the life we begin with a scream
we end with a whisper

Bucky Sinister, "The House that Punk Built"

In the meantime, if you demand on the one hand,
the raw material of poetry in
all its rawness and
that which is on the other hand
genuine, you are interested in poetry.

Marianne Moore, "Poetry"

The Poetry Oracle

The Lady is a humble thing
Made of death and water
The fashion is to dress it plain
And use the mind for border.

Elise Cowen, "The Lady..."

So sat I between the word truth
And the word fable
Took out my empty bowl
And spoon.

Charles Simic, "Pastoral"

I must go to the mountains
to hear
the sound and the sound.

Kijo Song, "Sound"

The Poetry Oracle

To drift with every passion till my soul
Is a stringed lute on which all winds can play,
Is it for this that I have given away
Mine ancient wisdom, and austere control?

Oscar Wilde, "Helas"

And graven with diamonds in letters plain
There is written, her fair neck round about,
"Noli me Tangere, for Caesar's I am,
And wild for to hold, though I seem tame."

Sir Thomas Wyatt The Elder, "Whoso List to Hunt"

There is neither heaven nor
earth,
Only snow
Falling incessantly.

Hashin, "The First Snow Of The Year"

I cannot abide these malapert males,
Pirates of love who know no duty

Sir William Davenant, from "Plays and Masques"

That if gold ruste, what shal iren do?

Geoffrey Chaucer, from "The General Prolouge, Canterbury Tales"

And cannot pleasures, while they last,
Be actual unless, when past,
They leave us shuddering and aghast,
With anguish smarting?

Lewis Carroll, "A Valentine"

Know you faire on what you look;
  Divinest love lyes in this booke

Richard Cranshaw, "On Mr. George Herberts booke intitued the Temple of
Sacred Poems, sent to a Gentle-woman"

look within

O get thee wings!

Henry Vaughan,
"The Brittish Church"

Doing, a filthy pleasure is, and short;
  And done, we straight repent us of the sport

Petronius Arbiter, "Doing, a filthy pleasure is, and short"

Wine comes in at the mouth
And love comes in at the eye

William Butler Yeats, "A Drinking Song"

Rich men, trust not in wealth,
    Gold cannot buy you health

Thomas Nashe, "Adieu, Farewell, Earth's Bliss"

Something sinister in the tone
Told me my secret must be known

Robert Frost, "Bereft"

The Poetry Oracle

Come in the evening, or come in the morning;
Come when you're look'd for, or come without warning.

Thomas Osbourne Davis, "The Welcome"

Here at our sea-washed, sunset gates shall stand
A mighty woman with a torch, whose flame
Is the imprisoned lightning, and her name
Mother of Exiles.

Emma Lazarus, "The New Colossus"

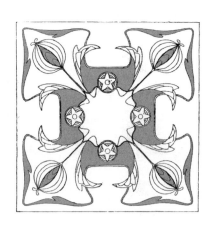

There are no people
To gape at them now,
For people are loth to
Peer in the dimness

Padraic Colum, "Monkeys"

The Poetry Oracle

The least flower with a brimming cup may stand,
    And share its dew-drop with another near.

Elizabeth Barrett Browning, "Work"

This cynic smile
  Is but a wile
  Of guile!
This costume chaste
  Is but good taste
  Misplaced!

W. S. Gilbert, "If You're Anxious for to Shine in the High Aesthetic Line"

The pulp so bitter, how shall taste the rind?

Francis Thompson, "The Hound of Heaven"

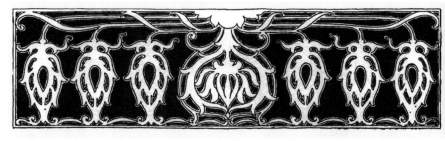

O drinke to thirst, and thirst to drinke that treasuer,
where the onely danger is to keepe a measuer.

William Alabaster, "Sonnet 32"

You did not come,
And marching Time drew on, and wore me numb.

Thomas Hardy, "A Broken Appointment"

And in his mistress' flame, playing like a fly,
Turned to cinders by her eye:
Yes; and in death, as life, unblessed,
To have it expressed,
Even ashes of lovers find no rest.

Ben Jonson, "The Hourglass"

The Poetry Oracle

**Who call me
as I go farther into emptiness**

Seuk Ho, "Something Greater Than Heaven"

There is a channel between voice and presence,
 a way where information flows.
In disciplined silence the channel opens.
With wandering talk, it closes.

Rumi, "Afghanistan"

How happy he, who free from care
The rage of courts, and noise of towns;
Contented breathes his native air,
In his own grounds.

Alexander Pope, "Ode on Solitude"

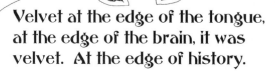

Velvet at the edge of the tongue,
at the edge of the brain, it was
velvet. At the edge of history.

Diane di Prima, "For Pigpen"

The tumult and the shouting dies;
   The Captains and the Kings depart:
Still stands Thine ancient sacrifice,
   An humble and a contrite heart.

Rudyard Kipling, "Recessional"

And the greatest gift
   God can give is His own experience.

Meister Eckhart, "Germany"

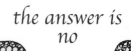

*the answer is
no*

usie old foole, unruly Sunne,
Why dost thou thus,
Through windowes, and
through curtaines call on us?

John Donne, "The Sun Rising"

And if I should live to be
The last leaf upon the tree
In the spring,
Let them smile, as I do now,
At the old forsaken bough
Where I cling.

Oliver Wendell Holmes, "The Last Leaf"

Not good for the land, not good for the sea
There's nothing biodegradable about it
But it does make one hell of an outfit.

Jessyka Stinston, "Tinsel Me Pretty"

That now are wild, and do not remember
That sometime they put themselves in danger
To take bread at my hand; and now they range,
Busily seeking with a continual change.

Sir Thomas Wyatt The Elder, "They flee from Me"

Can there be any day but this,
Though many sunnes to shine endeavour?
We count three hundred, but we misse:
There is but one, and that one ever.

George Herbert, "Easter"

Look what happens
to the scale
    when love holds it.
It stops working.

Kabir

A pattern, there she lay!
And so I stole her, read her,
Sleazily cajoled her
and was happy she was there.

Chris DeMento, "Letter from Georges
Budd to men of Beer Drinking Club"

But cease thy tears, bid ev'ry sigh depart,
And cast the load of anguish from thine heart:
From the cold shell of his great soul arise,
And look beyond, thou native of the skies

Phillis Wheatley, "To a Lady on the Death of Her Husband"

Who says that fictions only and false hair
Become a verse? Is there in truth no beauty?

George Herbert, "Jordan (1)"

Was for the abodes of cloudless day designed.

Judith Sargent Murray, "On the Equality of Sexes, Part I"

All we can touch, swallow, or say
aids in our crossing to God
and helps unveil the soul.

Saint Theresa of Avila, "Spain"

Man is a shop of ruses, a well truss'd pack,
Whose every parcell under-writes a law.

George Herbert, "The Church-porch"

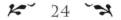

The church is put in fault;
The prelates been so haut,
They say, and look so high
As though they woulde fly
Above the starry sky.

John Skelton, "From Colin Clout"

But now, with New and Open Eyes,
see beneath, as if I were above the Skies

Thomas Traherene, "The Third Century"

Without sound we live in. Where
we are, really, climbing
the sides of buildings to peer in
like spiderman, at windows
not our own.

Diane di Prima, "My Lover's Eyes Are Nothing Like The Sun"

nd coward love, then, to the heart apace
Taketh his flight, where he doth lurk and plain,
His purpose lost, and dare not show his face.

Henry Howard, Earl Of Surrey, "Love, That Dough Reign and Live Within My Thought"

I find something greater emptied
Something greater than heaven emptied

Seuk Ho, "Something Greater Than Heaven"

Rash is the man, when the black banners blow,
Wha weds wi' the Queen o' the Castle o' Crow.

Helen Adam, "The Queen O' Crow Castle"

Green Buddhas
On the fruit stand.
We eat the smile
and spit out the teeth.
Charles Simic, "Watermelons"

When reading all those thick books on the life of god,
It should be noted that they were all written by men.

Bob Kaufman, "Heavy Water Blues"

She cries loudly for us to come! We hear,
for the night's many tongues
carry her cry across the sea.
Sappho, "To Atthis"

The Poetry Oracle

We who bear your creation seek re-creation.
Plant in your people a love and respect for your land.
Plant in your people a love and respect for your land.

Martin Palmer, "Listen To The Voices Of Creation"

Life smoothes us, rounds, perfects,
   as does the river the stone,
   and there is no place our Beloved is not flowing
   though the current's force you
   may not always
   like.

Saint Theresa of Avila, "Spain"

What? Not done complaining yet?

Anne Waldman, "A Phonecall From Frank O' Hara"

**All the false notions of myself that once caused
fear, pain, have turned to ash as I neared God.**

Hafiz, "Persia"

To goe to heaven, we maek heaven come to us.
We spur, we reine the starres, and in their race
They're diversely content t'obey our pace.

John Donne, "The First Anniversary. An Anatomy of the World"

Light came from the east, bright signal of God, the
sea became still so
that I might see the headlands, the windy walls of
the sea. Fate often
saves an undoomed man when his courage is good.

Beowulf, "The Feast at Herot"

ut Oh! What Human Fortitude can be Sufficient to Resist a Deity?

Aphra Behn, "A Congratulatory Poem"

Shall you have all or nothing
take half or pass by untouched?

Marge Piercy, "My Mother's Body"

Our passions help to lift us.
I loved what I could love until I held Him,
for then—all things—every world
disappeared.

Saint Theresa of Avila, "Spain"

The Poetry Oracle

The shell must break before the bird can fly.

Alfred Lord Tennyson, "The Ancient Sage"

it is certain

O kill kill kill kill kill
Those
Who advertise you
Out.

Charles Olson, "I, Maximus of Gloucester, To You"

And with a beck ye shall me call,
And if of one that burneth always
Ye have any pity at all,
Answer him fair with yea or nay.

Sir Thomas Wyatt The Elder, "Without Many Words"

**They seem anxious to know
What holds up heaven nowadays.**

James Merrill,
"After Greece"

*eat a meal &
ask again*

Like water
in goblets of
unbaked clay
I drip
out slowly,
and dry.
My soul
whirls. Dizzy.
Let me
discover my
home.

Lalla

God Damn you
God damn me
my
misunderstand-
ing of you.
Charles Olson,
"Moonset, Glouces-
ter, December 1, 1957,
1:58 a.m."

The Poetry Oracle

Alas! It is a fearful thing
To feel another's guilt!

Oscar Wilde,
"The Ballad of
Reading Gaol"

Next, sip this
weak wine
From the
green glass
flask, with its
    stopper.
Robert Browning,
"The Englishman in
Italy"

Even so you can
see in full dawn
The ground
there lifts
a foreign thing
desertless in
origin.
 A.R. Ammons, "Apologia
Pro Vita Sua"

The Poetry Oracle

A coin, a dot, the end of a sentence, the end of
the long improbable
utterance of the holy and human.

C.K. Williams, "The Modern"

e are resident inside the machinery,
a glimmering spread throughout the
apparatus.

Jack Gilbert, "Kunstkammer"

Twilight and evening bell,
And after that the dark!
And may there be no sadness of farewell,
When I embark.

Alfred Lord Tennyson, "Crossing the Bar"

The Poetry Oracle

You sing in my mind like wine. What you
did not dare in your life you dare in mine.

Marge Piercy, "My Mother's Body"

 rossed your bridge
with your big word
and your huge silence.

ruth weiss, "For Bobby Kaufman"

The teeming gulf-the sleepers and the shadows!
The past-the infinite greatness of the past!
For what is the present after all but a growth out of the past?

Walt Whitman, "Passage to India"

This piece of food cannot be eaten, nor this bit of
wisdom found by looking. There is a secret
core in everyone not even Gabriel can
know by trying to know.

Rumi

The worldy wisdome of the foolish man
Is like a Sive, that does, alone, retaine
The grosser substance of the worthless brain.

Francis Quables, "Book 2, Emblem VII"

Thy lust and liking is from thee gone.
Thou blinkard blowboll, thou wakest too late.

John Skelton, "Lullay, Lullay, Like a Child"

The Poetry Oracle

**These are the tranquillized Fifties
And I am Forty. Ought I to regret my seedtime?**

Robert Lowell. "Memories of West Street and Lepke"

you can be a good girl
and stop
telling everyone what you're doing
when you are abusing
drugs
and men
and bodies
that look something
like your own

perine parker, "denial"

Man is all symmetrie
Full of proportions, one limbe to another,
And all to all the world besides:
Each part may call the farthest, brother

George Herbert, "Man"

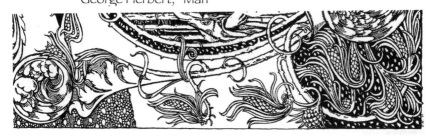

**None thither mounts by the degree
Of Knowledge, but Humility.**

Andrew Marvell, "A Dialogue, between the Resolved Soul, and Created Pleasure"

To rack old Elements,
Or Dust;
and say
Sure here he must
needs stay
Is not the way,
nor Just.

Henry Vaughan, "The Search"

This is
always the case.
Wherever I am
I am what is missing.

Mark Strand, "Keeping Things
Whole"

The Poetry Oracle

No darkness then did overshade,
But all within was Pure and Bright,
No Guilt did Crush, nor fear invade
But all my Soul was full of Light.

Thomas Traherne, "Innocence"

THE ONLY WAR THAT MATTERS IS THE WAR AGAINST
THE IMAGINATION

Diane di Prima, "Rant"

Suffering is what was born
Ignorance made me forlorn
Tearful truths I cannot scorn

Allen Ginsberg, "Don't Grow Old"

The Poetry Oracle

**Dear philosophers, I get sad when I think.
Is it the same with you?**
Charles Simic, "A Letter"

a spark of recognition and she
mouths the words takes his hand

G. Thomas, "warsaw"

This Planet will survive only if All
recognize a Common Mission

Norbert Korte, "There's No Such Thing As An Ex-Catholic"

She cries loudly for us to come! We hear,
for the night's many tongues
carry her cry across the sea.

Sappho, "To Atthis"

tonight I am the only one who knows me
and I hallucinate
I

eli coppola, "Who Am I To Say"

Isis is the original recycler.
She recycled her man, Osiris
And added a gold phallus
Rethink what you want to do.

ArtAmiss, "Isis"

f my desires, whereat I weep and sing,
In joy and woe, as in a doubtful ease,
For my sweet thoughts sometime do pleasure bring,

Henry Howard, Earl of Surrey, "Alas! So All Things Now Do Hold Their Peace"

I touch my palm. I touch it again and again.
I leave no fingerprint. I find no white scar.
It must have been something else,
Something enormous, something too big to see.

Charles Wright, "Equation"

"And know you not," says Love, "who bore the blame?
"My dear, then I will serve."
"You must sit down," says Love, "and taste my meat."
So I did sit and eat.

George Herbert, "Love"

he would rather have clean
sheets,
than my poem, but as long
as I don't bother her, she's
glad
to know I care.

Fleda Brown, "I Write My Mother a Poem"

The rage of courts, and noise of towns;
Contented breaths his native air,
In his own grounds.

Alexander Pope, "Ode on Solitude"

I hear the bells in the sky crying,
"Every being is blest."

Helen Adam, "Margaretta's Rime"

The leaves fall early this autumn, in wind.
The paired butterflies are already yellow with August
Over the grass in the West garden;
They hurt me.

Li Po, translated by Ezra Pound, "The River Merchant's Wife"

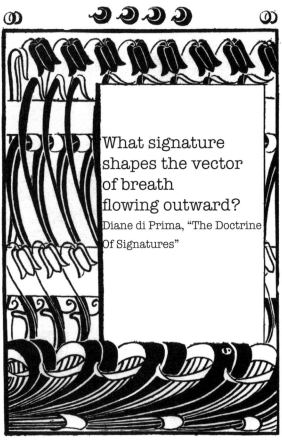

What signature
shapes the vector
of breath
flowing outward?
Diane di Prima, "The Doctrine
Of Signatures"

And, better yet
when the night
is over
she can curl
right up in her
dress and go to
sleep.
ArtAmiss, "What
Does It Matter?"

The Poetry Oracle

The ceremony of innocence is drowned;
The best lack all conviction, while the worst
Are full of passionate intensity.

William Butler Yeats, "The Second Coming"

For the river at Wheeling,
West Virginia,
Has only two shores:
The one in hell, the other
In Bridgeport, Ohio.

James Wright, "In Response To A Rumor That The Oldest Whorehouse In
Wheeling, West Virginia, Has Been Condemned"

We are but farmers of our selves, yet may,
If we can stocke our selves, and thrive, uplay
Much, much deare treasure for the great rent day.

John Donne, "To Mr Rowland Woodward"

The Poetry Oracle

Fade far away, dissolve, and quite forget
What thou among the leaves hast never known
The weariness, the fever, and the fret.

John Keats, "Ode to a Nightingale"

The people I love the best
jump into work head first
without dallying in the shallows
and swim off with sure strokes almost out of sight.

Marge Piercy, To Be Of Use"

If You wish me to leap joyfully, let me see
   You dance and sing –
Then I will leap into Love – and from Love
   into Knowledge, and from Knowledge
   into the Harvest, that sweetest Fruit
   beyond human sense.
   There I will stay with You, whirling.

Mechtild of Magdeburg

sleep on it & ask later

46

The Poetry Oracle

The wind goes nattering on,
Gossipy, ill at ease, in the damp room it will air.
I count off the grace and stays
My life as come to, and know I want less.

Charles Wright, "April"

What you do is how you get along
What you did is all it ever means.

Robert Creely, "Places to Be"

And on that cheek, and o'er that brow,
So soft, so calm, yet eloquent,
The smiles that win, the tints that glow,
But tell of days in goodness spent,
A mind at peace with all below,
A heart whose love is innocent!

Lord Byron, "She Walks in Beauty"

ust more waiting, with bells on,
And that Truth, is it only the FAC
  of WAITING,
    the flash at the end.

Elise Cowen, "Did I Go Mad?"

I said to God, "I will always be unless you cease to Be,"
  and my Beloved replied, "And I would cease to Be
  if you died."

Saint Theresa of Avila

And the more souls who resonate together,
  the greater the intensity of their love,
  and, mirror-like, each soul reflects the
  other.

Dante, "Italy"

et them smile, as I do now,
At the old forsaken bough
Where I cling.

Oliver Wendell Holmes, "The Last Leaf"

**The generations labor to possess
And grave by grave we civilize the ground.**

Louis Simpson, "To The Western World"

Now you feel how nothing clings to you;
your vast shell reaches into endless
space, and there the rich, thick fluids
rise and flow.

Rainer Maria Rilke

The Poetry Oracle

Your job is to find out what the world is trying to be.

William Stafford, "Vocation"

Presently my soul grew stronger,
hesitating then no longer.

Edgar Allan Poe, "The Raven"

I encourage blossoms to flourish with ripening fruits.
Hildegard of Bingen

The Poetry Oracle

There, in the windless night-time,
    The wanderer, marveling why,
Halts on the bridge to hearken
    How soft the poplars sigh.

A.E. Housman, "A Shropshire Lad"

We play in its skeletal maze
to find a warm rabbit
moving in a deep hole.

Louise Nayer, "Magic"

Get up and walk out into the first light.

Charles Simic, "Paradise"

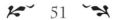

**I think I am going to climb back down
And open my eyes and shine.**

James Wright, "Lightning Bugs Asleep In The Afternoon"

May wide and towering heaven collapse upon me in all it
bronze and terror, catastrophe to the peoples of the eartl
on that day when I no longer stand by my companions,
on that day when I cease to harry my enemies.

Theognis of Megara

He held radical light
as music in his skull: music.

A.R. Ammons, "He Held Radical Light"

All poets pass,
but poetry remains.

Alberto Blanco, "Poem Seen in a Motel Fan"

Love alters not with his brief hours and weeks,
   But bears it out even to the edge of doom.

William Shakespeare, "Sonnet CXVI"

Love bade me welcome; yet my soul drew back,
Guilty of dust and sin.

George Herbert, "Love Bade Me Welcome"

nce
I saved my dreams
in a jar under my bed
for a week.
**Bucky Sinister, "The Little Children
Whom God Hated"**

I know what we call it
Most of the time.
But I have my own song for it,
And sometimes, even today,
I call it beauty.

James Wright, "Beautiful Ohio"

That wee-bit heap o' leaves an' stibble,
Has cost thee monie a weary nibble!
Robert Burns, "To a Mouse on Turning Her Up in Her Nest with
the Plough, November, 1785"

eed,
and not gratified
has helped me understand
why the suicide can do it
and the alcoholic can.

Rod McKuen, "Sleep After the Brighton Lanes"

The secret
Of this journey is to let the wind
Blow its dust all over your body.

James Wright, "The Journey"

I have no heart for wars I can't fight
Or bombs that destroy.

Joanna McClure, "Dear Lover"

The Poetry Oracle

HURRY UP PLEASE IT'S TIME

T.S. Eliot, "The Wasteland"

the answer is
yes

The age
Requires this task:
Create
A different image:
Re-animate
The mask.

Dudley Randal, "A Different Image"

All that we see or seem
Is but a dream within a dream.

Edgar Allen Poe, "A Dream Within a Dream"

The Poetry Oracle

Keep walking, though there's no place to get to.

Rumi

don't wait

I became You,
  Lord,
and forgot You.

Mahadeviyakka

There's no way out.
You were born to waste your life.
You were born to this middleclass life

Louis Simpson, "In the Suburbs"

What does not perish
Lives in thee.
Kenneth Patchen,
"There Is Nothing False In Thee"

Love me in the lightest part,
Love me in full being.
Elizabeth Barrett Browning,
"A Man's Requirements"

Let the night be too dark for me to see
Into the future. Let what will be, be.

Robert Frost, "Acceptance"

Futile the winds
To a heart in port—
Done with the compass,
Done with chart.

Emily Dickinson, "Wild Nights—Wild Nights!"

Even in the black waters
there is the luminescence
of one who has been saved.

Louise Nayer, "In The Islands"

We shall remember, when our hair is white,
These clouded days revealed in radiant light.

George Orwell, "Our Minds are Married But We are Too Young"

he state of man does change and vary,
Now sound, now sick, now blyth, now sary,

William Dunbar, "Lament for the Makers"

It is not fitted with a brake,
And endless are my verses,
Nor any yarn I start to make
Appropriately terse is.

Edward Dyson, "My Typewriter"

The Strangler's ear is alert for the names of Orpheus,
Cuchulian, Gawain, and Odysseus...

Kenneth Koch, "Fresh Air"

The Poetry Oracle

My first love gave me singing.
My second eyes to see,
But oh, it was my third love
Who gave my soul to me.

Sara Teasdale, "Gifts"

Once my life is Your gesture, how can I pray?

Mahadeviyakka

Don't panic
just keep it
Organic

Diamond Dave Whitaker

soon

Wild men who caught and sang the sun in flight,
And learn, too late, they grieved it on its way,
Do not go gentle into that good night.

Dylan Thomas, "Do Not Go Gentle Into That Good Night"

Sometimes you want
A vaguer touch: I understand
and won't give assertion up.

A.R. Ammons, "Working With Tools"

have faith

Nothing will be the same as once it was.

Weldon Kess, "Robinson"

The Poetry Oracle

A chorus of smiles, a winter morning.
Placed in a puzzling light, and moving,
Our days put on such reticence
These accents seem their own defense.

John Ashbery, "Some Trees"

The calm hand holds more than baskets of
goods from the market.

St. John of the Cross

My mother's countenance
Could not unfrown itself.

Theodore Roethke, "My Papa's Waltz"

One hour with thee! When sun is set,
Oh, what can teach me to forget
The thankless labors of the day;

Sir Walter Scott, "An Hour With Thee"

The darkness from the darkness. Pain comes from
the darkness
And we call it wisdom. It is pain.

Randall Jarrell, "90 North"

A basis rock-like of love & friendship
For all this world-wide madness seems to be needed.

John Berryman, "Of Suicide"

The Poetry Oracle

My roots are brandish'd in the heavens, my fruits in earth beneath.
Surge, foam and labour into life, first born and first consum'd!

William Blake, "Europe: A Prophecy Pendulum"

Illuminated in your infinite peace, a billion
  stars go spinning through the night

Rainer Maria Rilke

In a hummingbird's dance
there is no bird,
only movement.

Ok-Koo Kang Grosjean, "A Hummingbird's Dance"

**No one worth possessing
Can be quite possessed**

Sara Teasdale, "Advice to a Girl"

It is madness
says reason
It is what it is
says love

Erich Fried, "What It Is"

Let be be final of seem.
The only emperor is the emperor of ice cream.

Wallace Stevens, "The Emperor of Ice Cream"

The Poetry Oracle

And the angel in the gate, the flowering plum,
Dances like Italy, imagining red.

Louis Simpson, "Walt Whitman At Bear Mountain"

No love
No compassion
No intelligence
No beauty
No humility

Elise Cowen, "Unnamed"

We think by feeling. What is there to know?
I hear my being dance from ear to ear
I wake to sleep, and take my waking slow.

Theodore Roethke, "The Waking"

utside the open window
The morning air is all awash
with angels.
Richard Wilbur, "Love Calls Us To The
Things Of This World"

Where has fail'd a perfect return, indifferent of lies
or the truth?
Is it upon the ground, or in water or fire? or in the
spirit of man? or in the meat and blood?

Walt Whitman, "All Is Truth"

You have forty-nine days between
death and rebirth if you're a Buddhist.
Even the smallest soul could swim.

Maxine Kumin, "In The Park"

maybe

**Millions of observers guess all the
time, but each person, once, can say, "Sure."**

William Stafford, "My Father: October 1942"

Let it go inside of me and touch God.
Don't be shy, dear.
Every aspect of Light we are meant
to know.

St. John of the Cross

That night of time under the Christward shelter:
I am the long world's gentleman, he said.
And share my bed with Capricorn and Cancer.

Dylan Thomas, "Altar-wise by Owl-Light

**The calm soul knows more than anything
this world can offer from her beautiful womb.**

St. John of the Cross

the answer
is yes

Never seek to tell thy love,
Love that never told can be.

William Blake "Never Seek to Tell Thy Love"

Love likes a gander, and adores a goose.

Theodore Roethke, "I knew A Woman"

Don't try to see
through the distances.
That's not for human
beings.

Rumi

A poem spread
Across the Universe
To divine a prophecy
And affirm your
dream.

Brad Olsen, "speed poem, part 2"

everything changes

Let me see, then, what thereat is,
and this mystery explore,
Let my heart be still a moment
and this mystery explore.

Edgar Allan Poe, "The Raven"

O, may it be that far within
My inmost soul there lies
A spirit-sky, that opens with
Those voices of surprise?

William C. Gannett, "Listening for God"

If you can't be interesting at least you can be a legend

Frank O'Hara, "Yesterday Down At The Canal"

The cross is up with its crying victim, the clouds
Cover the sun, we learn a new way to lose.

Elizabeth Jennings, "Friday"

The Poetry Oracle

**And I see you and you're divine and I see you and you're a divine animal
and you're beautiful.**

Lenore Kandel, "Hard Core Love: To Whom it Does Concern"

And the man who feels superior to others,
that man cannot dance, the real dance.

St. John of the Cross

Ah, when to the heart of man
Was it ever less than a treason
To go with the drift of things,
To yield with a grace to reason,
And bow and accept the end
Of a love or a season?

Robert Frost, "Reluctance"

**the core directed
to its essence.**

ruth weiss, "Something Current"

Who lives in these dark houses?
I am suddenly aware
I might live here myself.

Louis Simpson, "After Midnight"

O, unto the pine-wood
At noon of day
Come with me now,
Sweet love, away.

James Joyce, "Chamber Music"

The Poetry Oracle

I'd ne'er entangle
My heart with other fere,
Although I mangle
My joy by staying here

Arnaut Daniel, "When sere leaf falleth"

My hand knows a thing of two
(remember what turned the wheel? What melted away?)
I can ask it to pluck a rose,
I can ask it to try the doors of mystery.

John Malcolm Brinnin, "John Without Heaven"

I see, in evening air,
How slowly dark comes down on what we do.

Theodore Roethke, "In Evening Air"

*the answer is
no*

A woman like that is misunderstood.
I have been her kind.

Anne Sexton, "Her Kind"

Imagine it, a Sophocles complete,
The lost epic of Homer, including no doubt.
His notes, his journals, and his observations
On blindness.

Theodore Weiss, "The Fire at Alexandria"

We speak the literal to inspire
The understanding of a friend.

Robert Frost, "Revelation"

The Poetry Oracle

**God blooms from the shoulder of the
elephant who becomes courteous
to the ant.**

Hafiz

No one saw your ghostly
Imaginary lover
State through the window,
And tighten
The scarf at his throat.

Robert Lowell, "The Old Flame"

How is this possible? How? Because divine love
cannot defy its very self.
Divine love will be eternally true to its own being,
and its being is giving all it can,
at the perfect moment.

Meister Eckhart, "Germany"

It is most true that the eyes are formed to serve
The inward light, and that the heavenly part.

Sir Philip Sidney, "From Astrophil and Stella"

Need Is Not Quite Belief

Anne Sexton, "With Mercy for the Greedy"

My friend, the things that do attain
The happy life be these, I find:
The riches left, not got with pain;
The fruitful ground; the quiet mind

Henry Howard, Earl of Surrey, "My Friend, the Things That Do Attain"

The Poetry Oracle

If it but be a world of agony.'—
'Whence camest though & whither goest thou?
How did thy course begin,' I said, '& why?'

Percy Bysshe Shelley, "The Triumph of Life"

For only cool techniques
Can forge the blue-sheened steel
And train the sword-arm's skill.

Robert Conquest, "Art and Civilization"

What a gush of euphony voluminously wells!
How it swells!
How it dwells

Edgar Allan Poe, "The Bells"

If such a tincture, such a touch,
So firm a longing can impour,
Shall thy own image think it much
To watch for thy appearing hour?

Henry Vaughan, "Cock-Crowing"

except the bee
who in its gluttony
drank all the toxic
honey

Nic Meacham, "untitled"

Thy vows are all broken,
And light is thy fame.

Lord Byron, "When We Two Parted"

The Poetry Oracle

Tell fortune of her blindness;
Tell nature of decay;
Tell friendship of unkindness;
Tell justice of delay,

Sir Walter Raleigh, "The Lie"

try again

He knew it, instantly.
He consented, himself, to
The finality of
An event.

Margaret Avison, "For Tinkers Who
Travel on Foot"

In the groves of Africa from their natural wonder
The wildebeest, zebra, the okapi, the elephant,
Have entered the marvelous. No greater marvelous
Know I than the mind's
Natural jungle.

Robert Duncan, "An African Elegy"

Make feast therefore now all this live long day,
This day for ever to me holy is,
Poure out the wine without restraint or stay,
Poure not by cups, but by the belly full.

Edmund Spenser, "Epithalamion"

If through the effect we drag the cause,
Dissect, divide, anatomize,
Results are lost in loathsome laws,
And all the ancient beauty dies.

Robert Lord Lytton, "The Artist"

Truth may seem, but cannot be,
Beauty brag, but 'tis not she,
Truth and Beauty buried be.

William Shakespeare, "The Phoenix and Turtle"

The Poetry Oracle

But words came halting forth wanting Invention's stay;
Invention, Nature's child, fled step-dame Study's blows,
And others' feet still seemed but strangers in my way.
Thus great with child to speak, and helpless in my throes,
"Fool," said my muse to me, "look in thy heart and write."

Sir Philip Sidney, "From Astrophil and Stella"

Some winter nights impel us to take in
Whatever lopes outside, beastly or kind.

William Meredith, "On Falling Asleep by Firelight"

Venemous thorns that are so sharp and
keen
Bear flowers, we see, full fresh and
fair of hue:
Poison is also put in medicine.

Sir Thomas Wyatt, "Pleasure Mixed With Pain"

Think of the still and the flowing

Edwin Honig, "November Through a Giant Copper Branch"

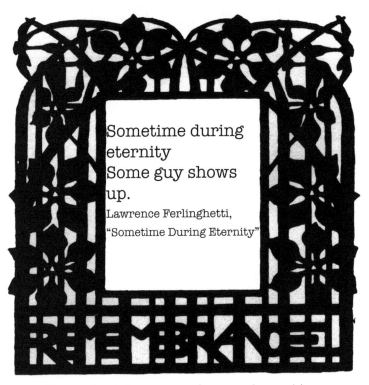

Sometime during
eternity
Some guy shows
up.
Lawrence Ferlinghetti,
"Sometime During Eternity"

I tell myself it's dark here on the peak and keeps on
getting darker.
It seems I am experiencing a kind of ecstasy.

Weldon Kess, "Robinson"

The Poetry Oracle

You could say
we live in
a life vest mentality
swim for life.

Anne Waldman, "I Am The Guard!"

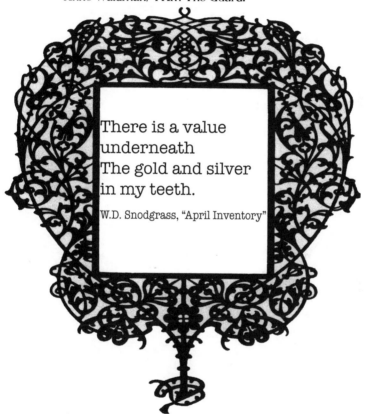

There is a value
underneath
The gold and silver
in my teeth.

W.D. Snodgrass, "April Inventory"

I am the breeze that nurtures all green.

Hildegard of Bingen

The Poetry Oracle

I planted you and I will pluck you
When it's time, said the Lord.

Mary Fabili, "From the Lord and Shingles"

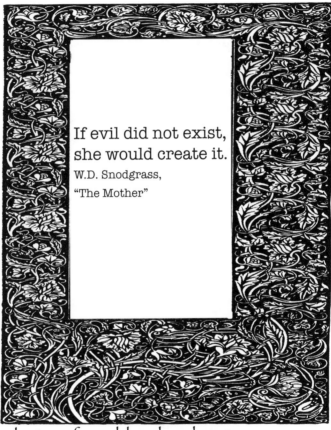

If evil did not exist,
she would create it.

W.D. Snodgrass,
"The Mother"

The glories of our blood and state
Are shadows, not substantial things,
There is no armour against fate,
Death lays his icy hand on Kings.

James Shirley, "Dirge"

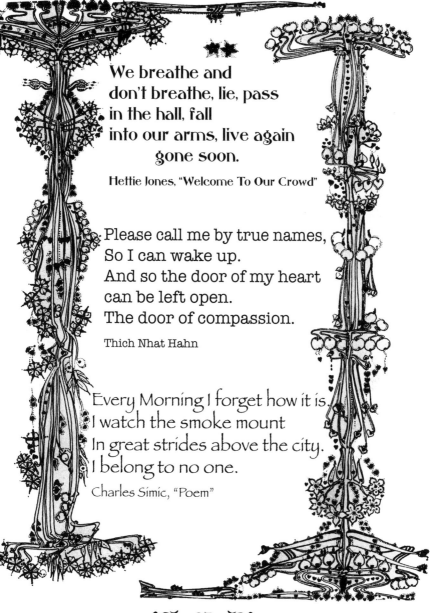

We breathe and
don't breathe, lie, pass
in the hall, fall
into our arms, live again
gone soon.

Hettie Jones, "Welcome To Our Crowd"

Please call me by true names,
So I can wake up.
And so the door of my heart
can be left open.
The door of compassion.

Thich Nhat Hahn

Every Morning I forget how it is.
I watch the smoke mount
In great strides above the city.
I belong to no one.

Charles Simic, "Poem"

The Poetry Oracle

Gather ye rosebuds while ye may,
Old time is still a-flying

Robert Herrick, "To the Virgins, To Make Much of Time"

*the answer is
most definitely*

You ask
Why I perch
On a jade green
mountain?

Li Po

No virtue can be thought to have priority
Over this endeavor to preserve one's being.

W.D. Snodgrass, "After Experience Taught Me"

The Poetry Oracle

I saw Eternity the other night:
Like a great ring of pure and endless light,
All calm as it was bright.

Henry Vaughan, "The World"

**when they scraped me clean
of you
i pretended
i had done this before.**

perine parker, "abortive reasoning"

I swear the earth shall surely be complete to him or
Her who shall be complete.

Walt Whitman, "A Song of the Rolling Earth"

ome live with me and be my love,
And we will come new pleasures prove,
Of golden sands and crystal brooks,
With silken lines and silver hooks.

John Donne, "The Bait"

Once drinking deep of the divinest anguish,
How could I seek the empty world again?

Emily Bronte, "Remembrance"

I would I could adopt your will,
See with your eyes, and set my heart
Beating by yours.

Robert Browning, "Two in the Campagna"

sk me no more where those starres light,
That downwards fall in the dead of night;
For in your eyes they sit, and there,
Fix'ed become as in their sphere.

Thomas Carew, "Song"

I would rather thou shouldst painfully repent,
Than by my threatenings rest still innocent.

John Donne, "The Apparition"

Pure of heart! thou needest not ask of me
What this strong music in the soul may be!

Samuel Taylor Coleridge, "Dejections: An Ode"

outcome likely

The day we die
The wind comes down
To take away
Our footprints.

Southern Bushmen

O hell, what do mine eye
with grief behold

Gary Snyder, "Milton By Firelight

Wet your whistle with wine now, for the dog star,
wheeling up the
sky,
brings back the summer.

Alcaeus of Mytilene, "Winter Scene"

The Poetry Oracle

Of the wide world I stand alone, and think
Till love and fame to nothingness do sink.

John Keats, "When I Have Fears That I May Cease to Be"

Music, when soft voices die,
Vibrates in the memory.

Percy Bysshe Shelley, "Music, When Soft Voices Die"

Wait upon it for
The edge only it
Gives.

Joanna McClure,
"Hard Edge"

ven such is time, which takes in trust
Our youth, our joys, and all we have,
And pays us but with age and dust,
Who in the dark and silent grave
When we have wandered all our ways
Shuts up the story of our days,
And from which earth, and grave, and dus[
The lord shall raise me up, I trust.

Sir Walter Raleigh, "The Author's Epitaph, Made by Himself"

Nothing is free
and in this truth
lies the reality
that freedom is nothingness.

Nic Meacham, "Free"

Beautiful and wild, the hawks, and men that are dying,
remember him.

Robinson Jeffers, "Hurt Hawks"

hese two were rapid falcons in a snare,
Condemned to do the flitting of the bat.

George Meredith,

"Thus Piteously Love Close What He Begat"

I grow old...I grow old...
I shall wear the bottoms of my trousers rolled.

Thomas Stearns Eliot," The Love Song of J. Alfred Prufrock"

When we would go moving as people do with
purpose would take apart this room stone
by stone and set ourselves outdoors
to mate with the sun.

Norbert Korte, "The Room Within"

The Poetry Oracle

**What is this life if, full of care,
We have no time to stand and stare.**

William Henry Davies, "Leisure"

Twelve nations
Bleed. Because I love, because
I need cherries, I cannot help them. My happiness,
bought cheap, must last forever.

Lucien Stryk, "Cherries"

I am the rain coming from the dew that causes the
grasses to laugh with joy of life.

Hildegard of Bingen

There, like the wind through woods in riot,
Through him the gale of life blew high.

Alfred Edward Housman, "On Wenlock Edge"

With bars they blur the gracious moon,
And blind the goodly sun:
And they do well to hide their Hell,
For in it things are done.

Oscar Wilde, "The Ballad of Reading Gaol"

Out of me unworthy and unknown
The vibrations of deathless music.

Edgar Lee Masters, "Anne Rutledge"

The Poetry Oracle

When the mind becomes Your mind,
  what is left to remember?

Mahadeviyakka

Better by far you should forget and smile
Than that you should remember and be sad.

Christina Georgina Rossetti, "Remember"

But like everyone else I learned
each time nothing new, only that
as it were, a music, however harsh, that held us
however lossely, had stopped, and left
a heavy thick silence in its place.

Denise Levertov, "The Dead"

The Poetry Oracle

what well have you
crawled out of
what wall
have you
recalled

perine parker, "backsliding
daughters"

From perfect grief there need not be
Wisdom or even memory.

Dante Gabriel Rossetti, "The Woodspurge"

But fly our paths, our feverish contact fly!
For strong the infection of our mental strife.

Matthew Arnold, "The Scholar-Gipsy"

After hours of
giddy drinking
and wild abandon
she found herself
under the table
in only her shoes!

ArtAmiss, "The Gift Bag"

correct to ❧ *proceed*

And the ground spoke when she was born.

Joy Harjo, "For Alva Benson, And For Those Who Have Learned To Speak"

Who hath not learned, in hours of faith,
The truth to flesh and sense unknown,
That life is ever lord of Death,
And Love can never lose its own!

John Greenleaf Whittier, "Snow Bound; A Winter Idyl"

**There she weaves by night and day
A magic web with colours gay.**

Alfred Lord Tennyson, "The Lady of Shallot"

They danced by the light of the moon,
The moon,
The moon,
They danced by the light
of the moon.
Edward Lear,
"The Owl and the Pussycat"

forgive

It isn't true about the lambs.
They are not meek.
Alice B. Fogel, "The Necessity"

hape nothing, lips; be lovely-dum

Gerard Manley Hopkins, "The Habit of Perfectio

Powered by words,
a company of voices.
In a fury he spins himself
turning upon the spit of his own burning rays,
and in a passion sings the room ablaze.

Madeline Gleason, "The Interior Castle"

When the bonny blade carouses,
Pockets are full, and spirits high,
What are acres? What are houses?
Only dirt, or wet or dry.

Samuel Johnson, "A Short Song of Congratulation"

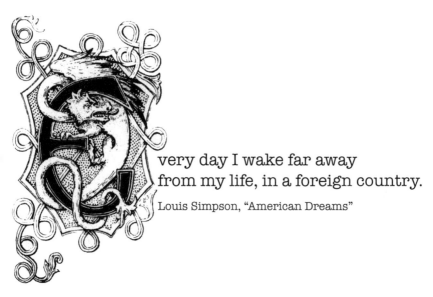

very day I wake far away
from my life, in a foreign country.

Louis Simpson, "American Dreams"

Little think'st thou
That thou to morrow, ere that Sunne doth wake,
Must with this Sunne, and me a journey take.

John Donne, "The Blossome"

The living record of your memory.
'Gainst death and all-obvious enmity
Shall you pace forth; your praise shall still find room
Even in the eyes of all prosperity
That wear this world out to the ending doom.
So, till the judgment that yourself arise,
You live in this, and dwell in lovers' eyes.

William Shakespeare, "Sonnet 55"

be   true

Knowledge always deceives. It always limits the Truth, every concept and image does.
Meister Eckhart

The sun may set and rise: But we contrarywise Sleep after ou short light One everlasting night.
Sir Walter Raleigh, "From The History O The World"

All extremes must meet; As some old poet has said: Out of a little earth And heaven, was Adam made.
Madeline Gleason, "Lyrics"

This morning I learned
There are no birds in Guam.
How come?

Mary Fabili, "From Second Monday in
May 1988"

Men at forty
Learn to close softly
The doors to rooms they will not be
Coming back to.

Donald Justice, "Men At Forty"

SUTTER MARIN swam in PLAYA ANGEL
made a pact with the angels
all mad to be reborn.

ruth weiss, "Post-card 1995"

Fearing making guilt making shame
    Making fantasy and logic and game and
    Elegance of covering splendour
    Emptying memory of the event.

Elise Cowen, "Teacher–Your Body My Kabbalah"

All you need to do is
look good, and show a
little skin.

Jessyka Stinston, "Vine Goddess"

Ill fares the land, to hastening ills a prey,
Where wealth accumulates and men decay.

Oliver Goldsmith, "The Deserted Village"

Man is all symmetrie
Full of proportions, one limbe to another,
And all to all the world besides:
Each part may call the farthes, brother.

George Herbert, "Man"

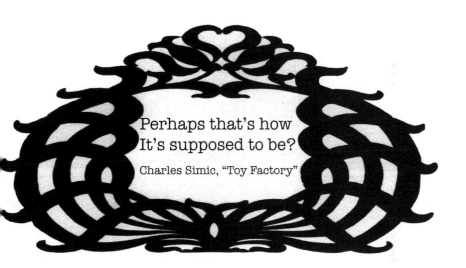

Perhaps that's how
It's supposed to be?

Charles Simic, "Toy Factory"

Who on Love's seas more glorious wouldst appear?
Like untuned golden strings all women are,
Which long time lie untouched, will harshly jar.
Vessels of brass, oft handled, brightly shine.

Christopher Marlowe, "Hero and Leander"

Only that Illumined One who keeps
   seducing the formless into form
   had the charm to win my
   heart.

Hafiz

A rain of tears, a cloud of dark disdain,
Hath done the wearied cords great hinderance.

Sir Thomas Wyatt the Elder, "My Galley"

She ran away in everybody's dreams
calling out like a booming flame
running running into the lines
of bards and lions lovers and birds
running with her arms out wide
into the bright flapping dark.

Norbert Korte, "Eddie Mae The Cook Dreamed Sister Mary Ran Off
With Allen Ginsberg"

H e loves to sit and hear me sing,
Then, laughing, sports and plays with me;
Then stretches out my golden wing,
And mocks my loss of liberty.

William Blake, "How Sweet I Roam'd from Field to Field"

"In my youth," father William replied to his son,
"I feared it might injure the brain;
But, now that I'm perfectly sure I have none,
Why, I do it again and again."

Lewis Carroll, "You Are Old, Father William"

Be still, I am content,
Take back your poor compassion
Joy was a flame in me
Too steady to destroy.

Sara Teasdale, "The Answer"

The Poetry Oracle

To your eyes, ears, and tongue, and every part.
If then your body go, what need you a heart?

John Donne, "The Blossom"

In the end the devil
He always wins
You think you can
out run him
But Lord how he
can swim.

A. Rae, "Heed"

True love in every moment praises God. Longing love
brings a sorrow sweet to the pure. Seeking love
belongs to itself alone. Understanding love
gives itself equally to all. Enlightened love
is mingled with the sadness of the world.

Mechtild of Magdeburg

The Poetry Oracle

Sad true lover never find my grave
To weep there.

William Shakespeare, from "Twelfth Night"

I laugh
But say
nothing
My heart
Free
Like a
peach
blossom.

Li Po

—Live television of what—is a lie.

Charles Olson, "A Later Note On Letter #15"

The Poetry Oracle

Exterminator does his job, takes his
money, leaves. In the long run of
things, he knows who will survive.

Lucien Stryk, "Exterminator"

But don't worry!   What must come, comes.
Face everything with love, as your mind
    dissolves in God.

Lalla, translated by Coleman Barks

One word is too often profaned
For me to profane it,
One feeling too falsely disdained
For thee to disdain it.

Percy Bysshe Shelley, "One Word Is Too Often Profaned"

The night knows nothing of the chants of night
It is what is is as
I am what I am.

Wallace Stevens

And lives go on.
And lives go on.
Like sudden lights
At street corners.

Donald Justice, "Bus Stop"

I love the dark race of poets,
And yet there is also happiness.
Happiness
If I can stand it, I can stand anything.

Louis Simpson, "Luminous Night"

If all the world and love were young,
And truth in every shepherd's tongue,
These pretty pleasure might me move
To live with thee, and be thy love.

Sir Walter Raleigh, "The Nymph's Reply"

I am led by the spirit to feed the purest streams.

Hildegard of Bingen

And that each thing exactly represents itself, and what has preceded it.

Walt Whitman, "All Is Truth"

The Poetry Oracle

**And now we talk of the "inner life,"
And I ask myself, where is it?**

Louis Simpson, "The Silent Piano"

If you have a spirit, lose it.
Lose it to return where
with one word,
   we came from.
Now, thousands of words,
   and we refuse to leave.

Rumi

*my sources
say yes*

Not marble, nor the gilded monuments
Of princes shall outlive this powerful rhyme;
But you shall shine more bright in these contents
Than unswept stone besmeared with sluttish time.

William Shakespeare, "Sonnet LV"

That I, above all, am chosen-even I
Must find that strange. I who was always
Disobedient, rebellious-smoked in the dining car.

W.D. Snodgrass, "The Fuhrer Bunker"

The whimpering airs that cry by night and never
find their rest
Are sobbing to be taken in and soothed upon my
breast.

Enid Derham, "The Wind-Child"

A fish cannot drown in water, a bird does not fall in air.
Mechtild of Magdeburg

The Poetry Oracle

How did the rose ever open its heart and
    give to this world all of its beauty?
It felt the encouragement of light against its being,
    otherwise we all remain too frightened.

Hafiz

But where is he, the Pilgrim of my song,
The being who upheld it through the past?

Lord Byron, CLXIV, from "Canto the Fourth, Childe Harold's Pilgrimage"

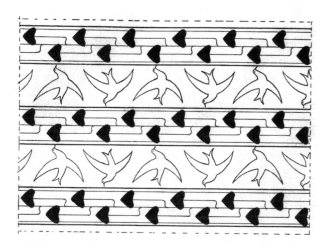

I admit to being, at times,
Suddenly, and without the slightest warning,
Exceedingly happy.

Charles Simic, "Heights Of Folly"

Best of all is to be idle,
And especially on a Thursday,
And to sip wine while studying
the light.

Charles Simic,
"Against Whatever It Is That's Encroaching"

I have always been at the same time
woman enough to be moved to tears
and man enough
to drive my car in any direction.

Hettie Jones,
"Untitled (Teddy Bears On The Highway")

When the mind is consumed with remembrance
of Him something divine happens to the
heart that shapes the hand and tongue
and eye into the word Love.

Hafiz

From cage to cage the caravan moves,
  but I give thanks, for at each divine
  juncture my wings expand and I
  touch Him more intimately.

Meister Eckhart

**Love touches love
the temple and the god
are one.**

Lenore Kandel, "God/Love Poem"

last chance

Each creature God made must live in its own true nature;
  How could I resist my nature, that lives for
  oneness with God?

Mechtild of Magdeburg

the
answer
is yes

Love alters not with his brief hour
and weeks,
But bears it out even to the edge
of doom.

William Shakespeare, "Sonnets CXVI"

And an old woman with a witch's stare
Cried "Praise the Lord!" She vanishes on a bus
With hissing air brakes, like an incubus.

Louis Simpson, "Hot Night On Water Street"

But selfless love bears an effortless fruit, working
so quietly even the body cannot say how it
comes and goes.

Mechtild of Magdeburg

The miracles that magic will
perform
Will make thee vow to study
nothing else.

Christopher Marlowe, "Dr Faustus. Act I"

belief

For we support all, fuse all,
After the rest is done and gone, we remain.

Walt Whitman, "As I Walk These Broad, Majestic Days"

But by and by the cause of my disease
Gives me a pang that inwardly doth sting,
When that I think what grief it is again
To live and lack the thing should rid my pain.

Henry Howard, Earl of Surrey, "Alas! So All Things Now Do Hold Their Peace"

The Poetry Oracle

Shall I compare thee to a summer's day?
Thou art more lovely and more temperate.

William Shakespeare, "Sonnet 18"

Sometimes afraid of reunion, sometimes of separation.
   You and I, so fond of the notion of a you and an I,
   should live as though we'd never heard
   those pronouns.

Rumi,

Bills, bills, bills
Thrills, thrills, thrills
Skills, skills, skills

Joanna McClure, "June 18, 1984"

find
yourself

maybe

Peace is always beautiful, The myth of heaven indicates peace and night.

Walt Whitman, "The Sleepers"

God, whose love and joy are present everywhere,
can't come to visit you unless you aren't there.

Angelus Silesius

For most men in a brazen prison live,
Where, in the sun's hot eye,
With heads bent o'er their toil, they languidly
Their lives to some unmeaning taskwork give

Matthew Arnold, "A Summer Night"

In the fire of its making, Gold doesn't vanish:
The fire brightens.

Mechtild of Magdeburg

Thy liberality, exceeds my power,
    Suffice it, that I thus record thy gifts,
    And bear them treasur'd in a grateful mind!

John Milton, "To My Father"

Be well assured that on our side
The abiding oceans fight

Rudyard Kipling, "A Song in Storm"

The Poetry Oracle

**As for the people—see how they neglect you!
Only a poet pauses to read the inscription.**

Louis Simpson, "Walt Whitman At Bear Mountain"

Quoth the Raven, "Nevermore."

Edgar Allen Poe, "The Raven"

How do I listen to others? As if everyone were
    my Master speaking to me his
    cherished last words.

Hafiz

The Poetry Oracle

Hope smiled when your nativity was cast

William Wordsworth, "Flowers On The Top Of The Pillars At The Entrance Of The Cav

outlook unclear

Wisdom is sweeter
than honey, brings
   more joy than
wine, illumines
more
   than the sun, is
more precious
   than jewels.

Makeda, Queen of Sheba

A flower unplucked is but left to the falling,
And nothing is gained by not gathering roses.
Robert Lee Frost, "Asking for Roses"

**I knuckled under, no regrets
but I've always wondered.**

Hettie Jones, "Sonnet"

look
within

Take of English earth
as much
As either hand may
rightly clutch.
In the taking of it
breathe
Prayer for all who lie
beneath.

Rudyard Kipling, "A Charm"

Birds make great sky-circles of their freedom.
How do they learn it? They fall, and
falling, they're given wings.

Rumi

Love is the funeral pyre where I have laid my living bod

Hafiz

No more be grieved at that which thou hast done:
Roses have thorns, and silver fountains mud.
Clouds and eclipses stain both moon and sun,
And loathsome canker lives in sweetest bud.

William Shakespeare, "Sonnet 35"

I say them, woman-who-signifies
I light the fire
I sit like a Buddha
I feed the animals outside the door
I blow out the lamp.

Anne Waldman, "Fast Speaking Woman"

The Poetry Oracle

**'Is thine own heart to thine own face affected?
Can thy right hand seize love upon thy left?**

William Shakespeare, "Venus and Adonis"

By the high verandah pillars, by the rotting bloodwood gates.

Crowded town or dreary seaboard, everywhere some woman waits!

M. Forrest, "The Lonely Woman"

Through love, through hope, and faith's transcendent dower,
We feel that we are greater than we know.

Alfred Lord Tennyson, "After-Thought"

The Poetry Oracle

The roses in the gypsy's window in a blue
vase, look real, as unreal.

Denise Levertov, "The Gypsy's Window"

Ironic, but one of the most intimate acts of our body is
death. So beautiful appeared my death - knowing
who then I would kiss, I died a thousand times
before I died.

Rabia

But O the heavy change,
now thou art gon,
    Now thou art gon, and
never must return!

John Milton, "Lycidas"

The Poetry Oracle

The difference between a good artist and a great one is:
The novice will often lay down his tool or brush then
pick up an invisible club on the mind's table and
helplessly smash the easels and jade.
Whereas the vintage man no longer hurts himself or
anyone and keeps on sculpting Light.

Hafiz

And olden memories
   Are startled from their long repose
   Like shadows on the silent snows

Abijah M. Ide, "To Isadore"

While the milder fates consent,
Let's enjoy our merriment.

Robert Herrick, "A Lyric to Mirth"

I Bring you with reverent hands
The books of my numberless dreams

William Butler Yeats, "A Poet to His Beloved"

in egypt
they tell the days
by the strings in their beads.

ruth weiss, "The Brink"

This poem is not addressed to you.
You may come into it briefly,
But no one will find you here, no one.
You will have changed before the poem will.

Donald Justice, "Poem"

The Poetry Oracle

**The sky is always ours,
even though we are crowded together.**

Louise Nayer, "Dream of the Uninterrupted Moss"

And out-lived illusions rise,
  And the soft leaves of the landscape
  Open on my thoughtful eyes.

Jennings Carmichael, "An Old Bush Road"

I am the yearning for good.
Hildegard of Bingen

The Poetry Oracle

Only a moment, as clocks can reckon,
Dwells the soul at that height of heights.

John Le Gay Brereton, "Middle Harbour"

And grateful, that by nature's quietness
   And solitary musings, all my heart
   Is softened, and made worthy to indulge
   Love, and the thoughts that yearn for human kind.

Samuel Taylor Coleridge, "Fears in Solitude"

Love is that that never sleeps, nor even rests, nor stays
   for long with those that do.
Love is language that cannot be said, or heard.

Rumi

**Only a Perfect One who is always
laughing at the word two
can make you know of
Love.**

Hafiz

I was delighted with myself, having offered
  everything I had; my heart my faith,
  my work.
"And who are you," you said, "to think you
  have so much to offer? It seems you
  have forgotten where you've come from."

Rumi

You in whose ultimate madness we live,
You flinging yourself out into the emptiness,
You- like us- great an instant,
O only universe we know, forgive us.

Galway Kinnell, "On Frozen Fields"

The Poetry Oracle

Look to the weather bow,
    Breakers are round thee;
Let fall the plummet now,
    Shallows may ground thee.

Caroline Bowles Southey, "Mariner's Hymn"

The woods are lovely, dark and deep.
But I have promises to keep

Robert Frost, "Stopping by Woods on a Snowy Evening"

All speaks of change: the renovated
    Forms
Of long-forgotten thins arise again.

Sir Humphry Davy, "Written After Recovery from A Dangerous Illness"

Such sailing and gilding,
Such sinking and sliding,
Such lofty curvetting,
And grand pirouetting
Richard Harris Barham,
"The Witches' Frolic"

So for this night I linger
here,
And full tossings too and
fro,
Expect still when thou
wilt appear
That I may get me up,
and go.
Henry Vaughn, "The Pilgrimage"

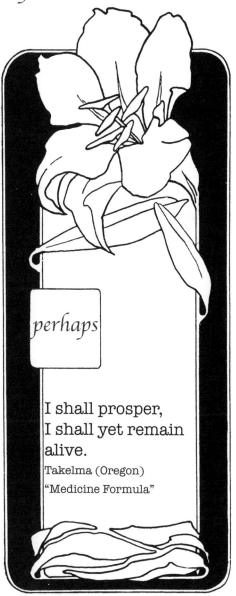

perhaps

I shall prosper,
I shall yet remain
alive.
Takelma (Oregon)
"Medicine Formula"

The Poetry Oracle

I watched you lay your athletes body down
Across the railroad earth
To make a bridge for souls

Helen Weaver, "For Jack"

The rest of my days I spend
wandering: wondering
what, anyway,
was that sticky infusion, that rank flavor of blood,
that poetry, by which
I lived?

Galway Kinnell, "The Bear"

Drumsound rises on the air, its throb, my heart.
A voice inside the beat says, "I know
   you're tired, but come. This is the way."

Rumi

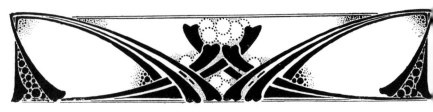

There is a Power whose care
Teaches thy way along that pathless coast.

William Cullen Bryant, "To a Waterfowl"

Found a family, build a state,
The pledged event is still the same.

Herman Melville, "Fragments of a Lost Gnostic Poem of the 12th Century"

Some for the Glories of This World; and some
Sigh for the Prophet's Paradise to come;
    Ah, take the Cash, and let the Credit go,
Nor heed the rumble of a distant Drum!

Edward Fitzgerald, "The Rubaiyat of Omar Khayyam"

The Poetry Oracle

**The way of love is not a subtle argument.
The door there is devastation.**

Rumi

all signs

point to yes

I am the self-consumer of my woes—
    They rise and vanish in oblivion's host

John Clare, "I Am"

Poetry, he don't work for the city.
He dumps your garbage onto a blank page.
You don't recognize it.
You call it beautiful.

Julia Vinograd, "From Poetry"

The Poetry Oracle

O, or that full bliss of though allied,
    Never to mortals given,
O, la thye lovley dreams aside,
    Or lift them unto heaven!

Felicia Hemans, "The Childe's Destiny"

Again!
   **Come, give, yield all your
strength to me!**

James Joyce, "A Prayer"

For we are the same things our fathers
    have been;
We see the same sights that our fathers
    have seen.

William Knox, "Why Should The Spirit of Mortal Be Proud?"

hildren can easily open the
drawer that lets
the spirit rise up and wear Its
favorite
costume of mirth and laughter.

Hafiz

We know nothing until we know everything.

St. Catherine of Siena

There is a garden in her face,
   Where roses and white lilies grow;
A heavenly paradise is that place,
   Wherein all pleasant fruits do flow.

Thomas Campian

ail divinest Melancholy,

Whose saintly visage is too bright
To hit the sense of human sight.

John Milton, "Il Penseroso"

Now let us sport us while we may,
And now, like amorous birds of prey,
Rather at once our time devour
Than languish in his slow-chapped power.

Andrew Marvell, "To His Coy Mistress"

**The lunatic, the lover, and the poet
Are of imagination all compact.**
William Shakespeare, "A Midsummer Night's Dream"

**Insects on a bough
floating downriver,
still singing.**

Issa, "In This World"

It is the rain
And all the sadness in the world
Won't make it stop.

Mary Fabili, "From the Priest"

I strive to mix some gladness with
my Strain,
    But the sad strings complain,
    And will not please the ear.

James Russell Lowell, "Commemoration Ode"

Loosened from the minor's tether;
Free to mortage or to sell.

Samuel Johnson, "A Short Song of Congratulations"

In moons and tides and weather wise,
He reads the clouds as prophecies.

John Greenleaf Whittier, "Snow-Bound; A Winter Idyl"

Cannibals love their food and don't hate anyone
Cannibals sing at the smell of dinner cooking
Listen to their happy music.

Julia Vinograd, "Cannibal Music"

The Poetry Oracle

**I do not own an inch of land,
But all I see is mine**

Lucy Larcom, "A Strip of Blue"

ask again later

The still air moves,
the wide room is less
dim.

Richard W. Gilder, "Dawn"

Slow, slow, fresh fount, keepe time with my salt teares

Benjamin Jonson, "Song"

What now?
any moment the question—
the only answer!

ruth weiss, "Single Out"

He thought as a sage, though he felt as
a man

James Beattie, "The Hermit" George

I bought a rose, a red, red rose.
Put it in a bottle and threw it out to sea.
Whoever finds it, there is no map.

Julia Vinograd, "Valentine"

Silence. Ashes
in the grate. Whatever it is
that keeps us from heaven,
sloth, wrath, greed, fear, could we only
reinvent it on earth
as song.

Galway Kinnell, "Last Song"

Those mortals with whom we couple or have coupled,
Clinging to our swan-suits, our bull-skins,
Our masquerades in coin and shrubbery.

Carolyn Kizer, "The Copulating Gods"

My Mind was once the true survey
Of all these Medows fresh and gay.

Andrew Marvell, "The Mower's Song"

The Poetry Oracle

You're in my eyes. How else could I see light?
You're in my brain. This wild joy.
  If love did not live in matter, how would any
  place have any hold on anyone?

Rumi

> But, present still, though now unseen,
>   When brightly shines the prosperous
>   Day,
> Be thoughts of thee a cloudy screen,
>   To temper the deceitful ray.

Sir Walter Scott, "Hymn of the Hebrew Maid"

Lord, you are my lover, my longing,
  my flowing stream, my sun,
  and I am your reflection.

Mechtild of Magdeburg

h my Lord, the stars glitter
and the
eyes of men are closed.

Rabi'a

He that is grounded in astrology,
Enriched with tongues, well seen in minerals,
Hath all the principles magic doth require.

Christopher Marlowe, "Dr. Faustus. Act I"

The sea is calling, calling,
Along the hollow shore.
I know each nook in the rocky strand,
And the crimson weeds on the golden sand,
And the worn old cliff where sea-
pinks cling,
And the winding caves where the echoes
ring.

Unknown, 'The Fisherman's Summons"

ontent I live; this is my stay,--
 I seek no more than my
suffice.
I press to bear no haughty sway;
 Look, what I lack my mind
supplies.

William Byrd, "My Mind to Me a Kingdom Is"

By the distant rill the maple grove looks scattered;
By the deep mountain the lane of bamboos looks peaceful;
The thin mist swallows up the departing birds;
The thin mist of the sinking sun companions the homing cattle.

Yuan Hao-wen, "The Maple Grove"

Even after all this time the sun never says to the earth,
 "You owe me." Look what happens
with a love like that - it lights the
whole world.

Hafiz

The Poetry Oracle

But flattery never seems absurd;
The flattered always takes your word.

John Gay, "The Painter Who Pleased Nobody and Everybody"

Ask the animals, and they will teach you.
Ask the birds of air, and they will tell you.

Job 12:7-10, "Ask the Animals"

Ever let the fancy roam,
Pleasure never is at home.

John Keats, "Fancy"

In the summer rain,
the path has disappeared

Buson, "Green Leaves, White Water"

Her lips began to scorch,
That juice was wormwood to her tounge,
She loathed the feast

Christina Rossetti, "Goblin Market"

You can never bring in a wall.

William Shakespeare, "A Midsummer Night's Dream"

No one yet had invented ownership
Nor guilt nor time.

Lenore Kandel, "Enlightenment Poem"

Listen my children and you shall hear
The sound of your own steps
The sound of your hereafter

Patti Smith, "Notes for the Future"

Ah, not to be cut off, not through the slightest partition
shut out from the law of the starts.

Rainer Maria Rilke

The Poetry Oracle

**down the open hatch again
you silly liquid sap**

perine parker, "with daddy"

I plucked pink blossoms from mine apple-tree
      And wore them all that evening in my hair:
Then in due season when I went to see
      I found no apples there.

Christina Rossetti, "An Apple Gathering"

One need not
be a chamber
to be haunted
Emily Dickinson,
"Ghosts"

oddess's of Air, Isis, and
Athena
They will help you know that
you are

ArtAmiss, "fortune'

As though at hide-and-seek with Spring.
My inmost thoughts, who can know them?
Ties of friendship are hard to make.
Alone in my romance, alone in my fragrance,
The moon comes to look for me.

Chu Tun-ju, "A Single Plum Tree"

**Each new discovery as
Slow and quiet as a
Possum's front feet.**

Joanna McClure, "Collage"

rom a world composed,
closed to us,
back to nowhere, the north.

Denise Levertov, "Another Journey"

My Beloved is a steeped herb, he has
    cured me of life.
Mira belongs to Giridhara, the One who
    lifts all, and everyone says she is mad.

Mira

Observe your life, between two breaths.
Breath is a wind, both coming and going.
On this wind you have built your life –
    but how will a castle rest on a cloud?

Avicenna (Ibn Sina)

Dwell thou in endless Light,
discharged soul.
Sir Henry Wotton,
"Tears at the Grave of Sr. Albertus Morton"

Love is the funeral pyre where the
heart must lay
   its body.

Hafiz, "Persia"

Now, when he and I meet, after all
these years,
I say to the bitch inside me, don't
start growling.
Carolyn Kizer, "Bitch"

He who the sword
of heaven will bear
Should be as holy
as severe

William Shakespeare,
"Measure for Measure"

I want to burn here,
in the heart of the
flame,
in the middle of
your arms,
under the sun.

Katherine O'Brien, "untitled"

When the soul lies down in that grass,
the world is too full to talk about.

Rumi, translated by John Moyne and Coleman Barks

 ow this day you have ceased to see daylight.
Think only of what is good.
Do not think of anything uselessly.

Fox, "A Speech to the Dead"

What has risen from the tangled web of thought and sinew now shines with jubilation through the eyes of ange and screams from the guts of Infinite existence Itself.

Hafiz

The little tress, ownerless, blossom untended;
Above the waste of misty grass the ravens home for the night.
Here and there broken walls encircle ancient wells;
Erstwhile, each of these was someone's habitation.

Tai Fu-Ku, "The Little Peach Trees"

hould we our Sorrows in this
Method range,
Oft as Misfortune doth their
Subjects change

Henry King, "An Elegy Upon My Best Friend"

If you live on the breath, you won't be tortured
by hunger and thirst, or the longing to touch.
The purpose of being born is fulfilled in the
state between "I am" and "That."

Lalla

The nice rain knows its season,
It is born of Spring.
It follows the wind secretly into the night.
And showers its blessings, silently, softly, upon everything.

Li Po, "A Quiet Temple Thick Set With Flowers"

The Poetry Oracle

Time shall mult away his wings
   Ere he shall discover
In the whole wide world agen
   Such a constant Lover.

Sir John Suckling, "Sir J.S."

In this world
we walk on the roof
of hell,
gazing at flowers.

Issa, "In This World"

In the midst of plenty you have started out.

Chiricahua, "Song of Maturation"

The Poetry Oracle

If this belief from heaven be sent
If such be Nature's holy plan,
Have I not reason to lament
What man has made of man?

William Wordsworth, "Lines
Written In Early Spring"

Oh turn away those
cruel Eyes,
　　　The stars of my
undoing.

Thomas Stanley, "The Relapse"

I have lived on the lip
of insanity, wanting to
　　know reasons, knocking on a door.
It opens.
I've been knocking from the inside!

Rumi, translated by John Moyne and Coleman Barks

alate, the hutch of tasty lust,
Desire not to be rinsed with wine
Gerard Manley Hopkins,
"The Habit of Perfection"

To place You in my heart may turn
    You into thought.
I will not do that!
To hold You with my eyes may turn
    You into thorn.
I will not do that!
I will set You on my breath
So You will become my life.

Rumi, translated by Maryam Mafi & Azima Melita Kolin

Their father
the Sun
who brought them to life
spoke the word of taking us out
Zuni, "The Beginning, Part I" translated by Dennis Tedlock

Kings have locked their doors and
each lover is alone with his love.
Here, I am alone with You.
Rabi'a

But do not touch my heart,
and so be gone;
Srike deep thy burning arrow in

Abraham Cowley, "The Request"

Every man to the devil his own way
Every man to the devil he must go
Lizzy Lee Savage, "Every Man to the
Devil His Own Way"

Here is my aphorism of the da
Happy people are monogamou
Even in California. So how doe
the poem play.

Carolyn Kizer, "Afternoon Happiness"

Listen, if you can stand to.
Union with the Friend means
not being who you've been,
being instead silence: A place:
A view
where language is inside seein

Rumi

Any thought of release from
this life
   will wrap you only more
tightly
   in its snares.

Ly Ngoc Kiev

He fumbles at your spirit
As players at the keys.

Emily Dickinson, "The Master"

Is it for me to drink the sweet
water poured out
And all day sit idle?

Papago, "War Song"

Know the true nature of
your Beloved.
In His loving eyes your
every thought,
    word, and movement is
always,
    always beautiful.

Hafiz

The Poetry Oracle

Cut brambles long enough, sprout after
  sprout, and the lotus will bloom of
  its own accord:
Already waiting in the clearing, the
  single image of light.
The day you see this, that day
  you will become it.

Sun Bu-er

You look but cannot reach,
You walk, the road twisting.

Sung Dynasty, "Moments Of Riding Mist"

Know that love is a careless child
  And forgets promise past.

Anonymous, "As You Came from the Holy Land of Walsingham"

The Poetry Oracle

Wearing our gestures, how wise you grow,
ballooning to overfill our space,
the almost-parents of your parents now.
So briefly having you back to measure us
is harder than having let you go.

Maxine Kumin, "Family Reunion"

Not one is dissatisfied,
not one is demented
with the
       mania of owning
things.

Walt Whitman,
"I Believe A Leaf Of Grass"

you may rely on it

You are sufficient.
You are perfect wherever you are.
When powerful your splendor overflows
My eyes you little heaven.

Hyonsung Kim, "Light"

May it be beautiful
before me.
May it be beautiful
behind me.
May it be beautiful
below me.
May it be beautiful
above me.
May it be beautiful
all around me.
In beauty it is
finished.

Navajo, "A Prayer
of the Night Chant"

One hundred and sixty-five recycled coffee filters.
A lot of time
And a lot of glue.

Debbie Dean, "Sex Spresso"

My Love to Saints and Angels, things divine,
But in thy tender jealosy dost doubt
Least the World, Fleshe, yea Devill putt thee out.

John Donne, "Holy Sonnets, 17"

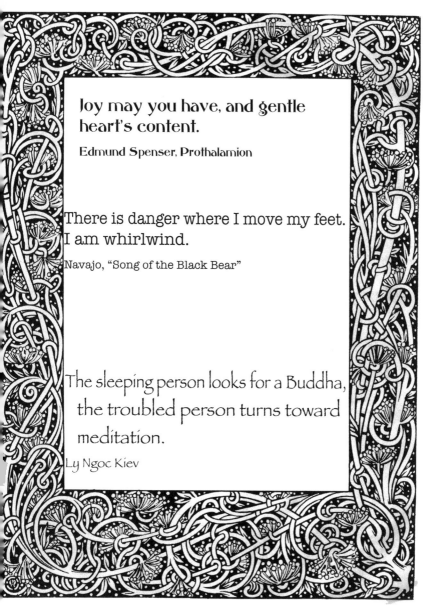

Joy may you have, and gentle heart's content.

Edmund Spenser, Prothalamion

There is danger where I move my feet. I am whirlwind.

Navajo, "Song of the Black Bear"

The sleeping person looks for a Buddha, the troubled person turns toward meditation.

Ly Ngoc Kiev

ind also in this sound a thought,
Hearing it by this distant northern sea.

Matthew Arnold, "Dover Beach"

May your road be fulfilled.
Reaching to the road of your sun father,
When your road is fulfilled,
In your thoughts may we live.

Zuni, "Prayer Spoken While Presenting An Infant to the Sun"

You speak to me of dangers that I may fear,
But I have willed to go, my friends.

Osage, "A Warrior's Song of Defiance"

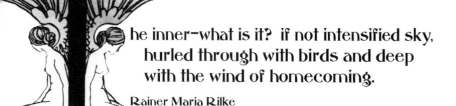

The inner—what is it? if not intensified sky,
 hurled through with birds and deep
 with the wind of homecoming.

Rainer Maria Rilke

I love her like a mother, and she embraces
 me as her own child. I will follow her
 footprints and she will not cast
 me away.

Makeda, Queen of Sheba

Mountains are steadfast but the mountain
 streams go by, go by, and yesterdays
 are like the rushing streams, they fly,
 they fly, and the great heroes,
 famous for a day, they die,
 they die.

Hwang Chin

Love bade me welcome: yet my soul drew back,
Guiltie of dust and sinne.

George Herbert, "Love (III)"

all signs point to no

Crescent moon-
bent to the shape
of the cold.

Issa, "In This World"

Spirits intoxicate
The drinker, not
the glass.

James Merrill, "Waterspout"

This mountain of release is such that the
   ascent's most painful at the start,
   below; the more you rise, the
   milder it will be.

Dante

**When shall the traveller
come home,
     That will not move?**

Henry Vaughan, "The Resolve"

ask again

Not one kneels to one another, nor to this kind that
lived thousands
     of years ago,
Not one is respectable or unhappy over the whole earth.

Walt Whitman, "I Believe A Leaf Of Grass"

But the one who knows that there's
  nothing to seek knows too that
  there's nothing to say.
She keeps her mouth closed.

Ly Ngoc Kiev

When the words stop and you can
    endure the silence that reveals
    your heart's pain of emptiness
    or that great wrenching-sweet
    longing, that is the time to
    try and listen to what the
    Beloved's eyes most
    want to say.

Hafiz

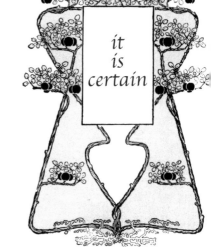

it
is
certain

Alas! it is a fearful thing
  To feel another's guilt!

Oscar Wilde, "The Ballad of Reading Gaol"

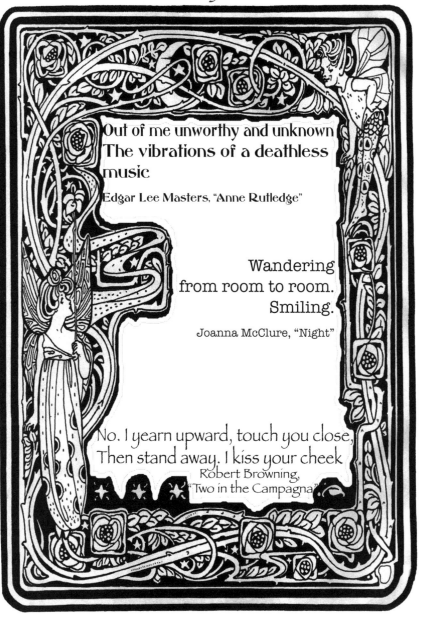

Out of me unworthy and unknown
The vibrations of a deathless
music

Edgar Lee Masters, "Anne Rutledge"

Wandering
from room to room.
Smiling.

Joanna McClure, "Night"

No. I yearn upward, touch you close,
Then stand away. I kiss your cheek
Robert Browning,
"Two in the Campagna"

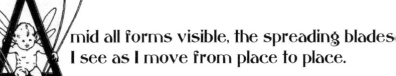

mid all forms visible, the spreading blades
I see as I move from place to place.

Osage, "The Song of the Maize"

And when the slope feels gentle to the point
that climbing up sheer rock is effortless
as though you were gliding downstream
in a boat, then you will have arrived
where this path ends.

Dante

The height of the adventure is the height
Of country where two village cultures faded
Into each other. Both of them are lost.

Robert Frost, "Directive"

And so time passes, passes by, passes over,
passes away and through and pass the butter,
please. Sometimes time passes by so fast
you can't even see those seconds make their
little streaks of re-entry into your heart.

Jan Kerouac, "Chapter 47"

From Cobblestone Gardens comes a pretty bird
Trapped in treacherous chicken wire, bird netting, and
flimsy fencing.

Debbie Dean, "Chicken Wire, Bird Netting & Flimsy Fencing"

Behind each eye here, one glowing
  weather.

Rumi

The Poetry Oracle

How graceful the small before danger!

Theodore Roethke, "Meditation At Oyster River"

Nothing move thee; nothing terrify thee; everything passes.

Saint Theresa of Avila

Figuring it all out no problem
giving it all up no problem
giving it all way no problem
devouring everything in sight no problem.

Diane di Prima, "No Problem Party Poem"

The Poetry Oracle

Playfully you hid from me.
All day I looked.
Then I discovered
I was you, and the celebration
  of That began.

Lalla

the voices twisted
losing all meaning
so I waited wondering how long until it was over.
or when it would start all over again.

Jolene G., "Chaos"

Which is worth more, a crowd of thousands,
  or your own genuine solitude?
Freedom, or power over an entire nation?

Rumi

It's this simple
before I was with you
now I'm here.

Hettie Jones, "Rabbits, Rabbits, Rabbits"

And I died a hero's death
I sang in God's holy choir
I breathed a lonely dying breath
I died a hero's death

Lizzy Lee Savage, "A Hero's Death"

Sing, my tongue; sing, my hand;
sing, my feet, my knee,
my loins, my
whole body.
Indeed I am His choir.

St. Thomas Aquinas

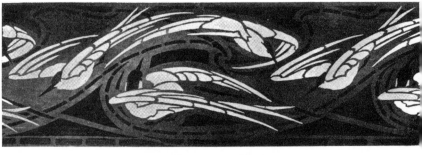

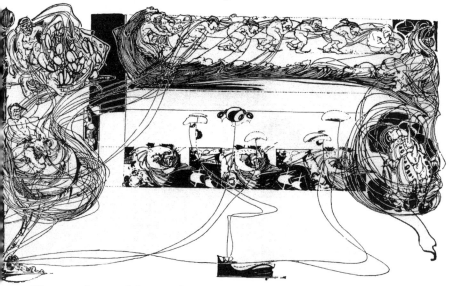

Every forest branch moves differently
  in the breeze, but as they sway
  they connect at the roots.

Rumi

I cannot lose anything in this place of
  abundance I found.

St. Catherine of Siena

Madam, two hearts we brake,
And from them both did take
The best, one heart to make.

Michael Drayton, "The Heart"

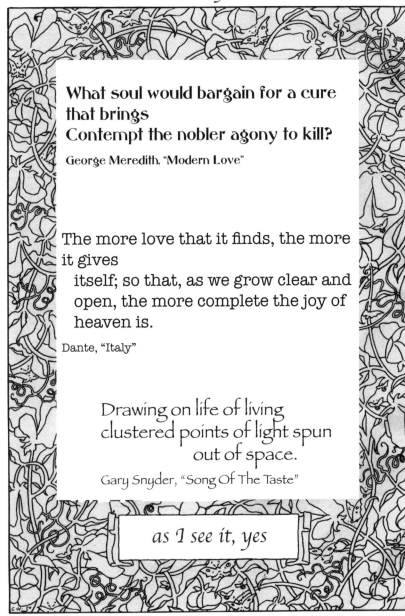

What soul would bargain for a cure that brings
Contempt the nobler agony to kill?

George Meredith, "Modern Love"

The more love that it finds, the more it gives
itself; so that, as we grow clear and open, the more complete the joy of heaven is.

Dante, "Italy"

Drawing on life of living
clustered points of light spun
out of space.

Gary Snyder, "Song Of The Taste"

as I see it, yes

I want to tell
what the forests
were like
I will have to
speak
in a forgotten
language.

W.S. Merwin, "Witness"

reply hazy

I came back to myself,
To the real work, to
        "What is to be done."

Gary Snyder, "I Went Into The Maverick Bar"

And here I am, the
center of all the beauty!
writing these poems!
Imagine!

Frank O'Hara, "Autobiographia Literaria"

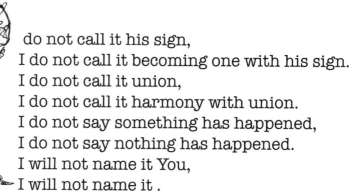

do not call it his sign,
I do not call it becoming one with his sign.
I do not call it union,
I do not call it harmony with union.
I do not say something has happened,
I do not say nothing has happened.
I will not name it You,
I will not name it .
Now that the White Jasmine Lord is myself,
what use for words at all?

Mahdeviyakka

I have no patience for a longer stay,
But must go down
And leave the chargeable noise of this great town.

Thomas Randolph, "An ode to Mr. Anthony Stafford to hasten him into the country"

There is a desert I long to be walking,
a wide emptiness, peace beyond
any understanding of it.

Rumi

friends on this Path, my eyes are no
    longer my eyes.
A sweetness has entered through
them,
    has pierced through to my heart.

Mira

When I am Fifty shall my
face drift into those elongations
of innocence and confront me?

Frank O'Hara, "Poem"

The great sea has set me in motion,
    set me adrift, moving me like a
    weed in a river.

Uvavunuk, "Netsilik Eskimo"

Why should I share you? Why don't you get rid of someone else for a change?

Frank O'Hara, "Meditations In An Emergency"

I am looking for a poem that says
Everything so I don't have to
write anymore.

Tukuram

All things that love the sun are out of
doors;
The sky rejoices in the morning's birth
William Wordsworth, "Resolution and Independence"

The Poetry Oracle

Great expectation, wear a train of shame.

Sir Philip Sidney, "Astrophel and Stella"

Pain the soul, never mind the legs and
arms!

Robert Browning, "Fra Lippo Lippi"

A sweet disorder in the dress
Kindles in clothes a wantonness

Robert Herrick, "Delight in Disorder"

The Poetry Oracle

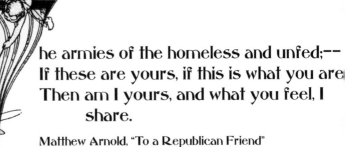

he armies of the homeless and unfed;--
If these are yours, if this is what you are
Then am I yours, and what you feel, I
share.

Matthew Arnold, "To a Republican Friend"

I can't believe there's not
another world where we will sit
and read new poems to each other.

Frank O'Hara, "To John Ashbery"

Out beyond ideas of wrongdoing and rightdoing,
there is a field. I'll meet you there.

Rumi, translated by John Moyne and Coleman Barks

hate'er you dream, with doubt possessed,
Keep, keep it snug within your breast

Arthur Hugh Clough, "All is Well"

I wish her store
Of worth may leave her poor.
Of wishes, and I wish—no more.

Richard Crashaw, "Wishes to his supposed mistress"

Mystical grammar of amorous glances;
Feeling of pulses, the physic of love;
Rhetorical courtings and musical dances;
Numbering of kisses arithmetic prove

John Cleveland, "Marc Antony"

are you here?
is he?
is she?
she is.
he is.
he is who?

ruth weiss, "Single Out"

Like a wind that sucks the sea,
    Over and in and on the sea,
Good sooth it was a mad delight;
And every man of all the four
Shut his eyes and laugh'd outright.

William Bell Scott, "The Witch's Ballad"

Agonies are one of my changes of garments
Walt Whitman, "Song of Myself"

The Poetry Oracle

Men are fools that wish to die!
Is't not fine to dance and sing
When the bells of death do ring?

Anonymous, "Hey Nonny No"

These have the spirit's range,
The measure of the mind.

C. Day Lewis, "In Me Two Worlds"

family is the key

Fie on sinful fantasy!
Fie on lust and luxury!
Lust is but a bloody fire,
Kindled with unchaste desire
William Shakespeare,
"The Merry Wives of Windsor"

Between living and dreaming
there is a third thing.
Guess it.

Antonio Machado

you
may
rely
on
it

Birth, old age, sickness, and death:
From the beginning, this is the
way things have always been.

Ly Ngoc Kiev

Some prisoned moon in steep cloud-fastness,--
   Throned queen and thralled; some dying sun whose pyre
   Blazed with momentous memorable fire;--
Who hath not yearned and fed his heart with these?

Dante Gabriel Rossetti, "The Soul's Sphere"

Tenants of the house,
Thoughts of a dry brain in a dry season.

T.S. Eliot, "Gerontion"

A wanderer is man
from his birth.
He was born in a ship
On the breast of the
river of Time

Matthew Arnold, "The Future"

try
love

The luscious and impeccable fruit of life
Falls, it appears, of its own weight to earth.

Wallace Stevens, "Le Monocle de Mon Oncle"

The Poetry Oracle

He shall be strong to sanctify the poet's high vocation

Elizabeth Barrett Browning, "Cowper's Grave"

sleep on it

Think of the language we two, same and not-same,
might have constructed from sign,
scratch, grimace, grunt, vowel:
Laughter our first noun, and our long verb, howl.

Maxine Kumin, "Nurture"

One instant is eternity; eternity is the now.
When you see through this one instant,
   you see through the one who sees.

Wu-Men

He who binds to himself a joy does the
   winged life destroy.
But he who kisses the joy as it flies
   lives in eternity's sun rise.

William Blake

There are moments when speech is but a mouth pressed
Lightly and humbly against the angel's hand.

James Merrill, "A Dedication"

I'll shed the tear of souls,
the true
Sweat, Blake's intellectual
dew,
Before I am resigned to slip
A dusty finger on my lip.

Stanley Kunitz, "Single Vision"

Without your
intellectual
and spiritual
Values, man,
you are sunk.

James Merrill, "Charles On Fire"

Aye! be silent! Let them each hear each other breathing
For a moment, mouth to mouth!

Elizabeth Barrett Browning, "The Cry of the Children"

I do not tell her, it would sound theatrical
Indeed this green room's mine, my very life.
We are each other's; there will be no wife;
The little feet that patter here are metrical.

James Merrill, "From Up and Down"

O heart of stone,
are you flesh, and
caught
By that you
swore
to withstand?
Alfred Tennyson, "Maud:
A Monodrama"

I am
fevered
with the
sunset,
I am
fretful
with the
bay
Richard
Hovey, "The
Sea Gypsy"

Pray but one
prayer for me
'twixt thy closed
lips,
    Think but one
thought of me
up in the stars.
William Morris, "Summer
Dawn"

The Poetry Oracle

In my travels I spent time with a great yogi.
Once he said to me, "Become so still you
  hear the blood flowing through your veins."
One night as I sat in quiet, I seemed on the
  verge of entering a world inside so vast
I know it is the source of all of us.

Mira

My soul is full of whispered song,—
  My blindness is my sight;
The shadows that I feared so long
  Are full of life and flight.

Alice Cary, "Her Last Poem"

This is my dwelling, this is my truest home:
A house of clay best fits a guest of loam.

William Austin, "Verse 13: Sepulchrm Domus Mea Est"

The Poetry Oracle

Oh, they'll never let a man be good,
    They whisper in his ear,
Until the fever heats his blood
    To see the big ships clear.

Leo Hays, "Ports of Call"

Crescendo, and agape on the crumbling ridge
Stand in a row and learn.

W.S. Merwin, "The Drunk In The Furnace"

Be you all pleased? Your pleasures grieve not me.
    Do you delight? I envy not your joy.
    Have you content? Contentment with you be.

Lady Mary Wroth, "Sonnet IX"

This morning, timely rapt with holy fire,
I thought to form unto my zealous muse
What kind of creature I could most desire
To honour, serve and love, as poets use.

Ben Jonson, "Epigram LXXVI: On Lucy, Countess of Bedford"

Tell me, you anti-saints, why glass
With you is longer lived than brass?

Richard Corbett, "Upon Fairford Windows"

Yet have I been a lover by report,
Yea, I have died for love as others do.

Sir Robert Ayton, "Upon Love"

The Poetry Oracle

It is the echo of divine silence we hear the birds sing, and that is the source of all we see and touch.

Tukaram

I was sad one day and went for a walk;
I sat in a field.
A rabbit noticed my condition and
  came near.
It often does not take more than that to
  help at times - to just be close to
  creatures who are so full of knowing,
  so full of love that they don't
  chat, they just gaze with their
  marvelous understanding.

St. John of the Cross

The spirit matters
Most of the words gone.

Joanna McClure, "Sappho"

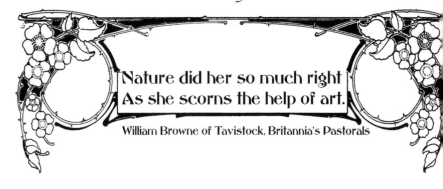

Nature did her so much right
As she scorns the help of art.

William Browne of Tavistock, Britannia's Pastorals

Our hands imbibe like roots, so I place them
   on what is beautiful in this world.
And I fold them in prayer, and they draw
   from the heavens light.

St. Francis of Assisi

Then let us have our liberty again,
And challenge to yourselves no sovereignty:
You came not in the world without our pain;
Make that a bar against your cruelty.

Emilia Lanier, "Salve Deus Rex Judaeorum"

The Poetry Oracle

The spade, for labour stands. The ball with wings
Intendeth flitting, rolling, wordly things.

George Wither, "The Spade"

Love built a stately house; where fortune came,
And spinning fancies, she was heard to say
That her fine cobwebs did support the frame.

George Herbert, "The World"

Spring overall. But inside us there's
another unity.

Rumi

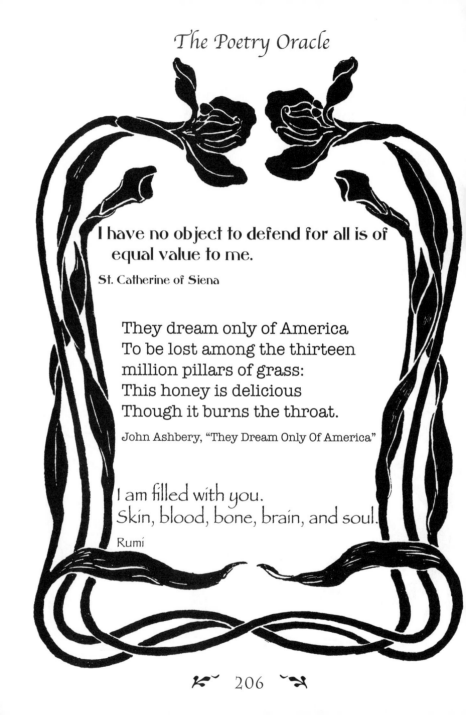

I have no object to defend for all is of equal value to me.

St. Catherine of Siena

They dream only of America
To be lost among the thirteen
million pillars of grass:
This honey is delicious
Though it burns the throat.

John Ashbery, "They Dream Only Of America"

I am filled with you.
Skin, blood, bone, brain, and soul.

Rumi

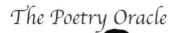

The Muses nine,
The nymphs divine,
Do all condole my woe.

George Chapman, "The Good Shepherd's Sorrow for
the Death of His Beloved Son"

Being is not what it seems, nor non-being.
The world's existence is not in the world.

Rumi

Love made me poet,
And this I writ;
My heart did do it,
And not my wit.

Lady Elizabeth Tanfield, "Epitath for Sir Lawrence
Tanfield"

The Poetry Oracle

As in those thick clouds which the glove enclose
Th'all-working spirit were yet again to wade,
And heaven and Earth again were to be made.

Michael Drayton, "Noah's Flood"

That which creates a happy life
Is substance left, not gained by strife

Mildmay Fane, Early of Westmorland, "A Happy Life"

I know how it will be when I die, my
beauty will be so extraordinary
that God will worship me.

Rabia

The Poetry Oracle

I used to have fiery intensity, and a
flowing sweetness.
The waters were illusion.
The flames, made of snow.
Was I dreaming then?
Am I awake now?

Rumi

In vain, fair sorceress, thy eyes speak charms,
In vain thou mak'st loose circles with thy arms.

William Habington, "To a Wanton"

Self inside self, You are nothing but me.
Self inside self, I am only You.
What we are together will never die.
The why and how of this?
What does it matter?

Lalla

The Poetry Oracle

This poem is concerned with language on a very plain level.
Look at it talking to you. You look out a window
Or pretend to fidget. You have it but you don't have it.
You miss it, it misses you. You miss each other.

John Ashbery, "Paradoxes And Oxymorons"

> Even I, while humble zeal
> Makes fancy a sad truth indite,
> Insensible away do steal;
> And when I'm lost in death's cold night,
> Who will remember, now I write?
>
> William Harington, "Solum Mihi Superest Sepulchrum"

He thinks the moon is a small hole at the top of the sky,
proving the sky a quite useless for protection.
He trembles, but must investigate as high as he can climb.

Elizabeth Bishop, "The Man Moth"

The furtive burrowing of birds
singing in a frail winter sun
quiet singing quiet.
Norbert Korte, "Throwing Firecrackers
Out The Window While The Ex-Husband
Drives By"

I searched for my Self until I grew weary,
but no one, I know now, reaches the
hidden knowledge by means of effort.
Then, absorbed in "Thou art This," I found
the place of Wine.
There all the jars are filled, but no one is
left to drink.

Lalla

I will skip a lot of what happens next.
Then the moment comes. Everything, everything
has been said, and the wheels start to turn.

Thomas Marvin Bell, "Ending With A Line From Lear"

hy should we doubt, before we go
To find the knowledge which shalle ver last,

That we may there each other know?
Can future knowledge quite destroy the past?

Sir William Davenant, "Song, Endymon Porter and Olivia"

All day and night, music, a quiet, bright reedsong. If it fades, we fade.

Rumi

And fools call Nature, didst hear, comprehend.
Accept the obligation laid on thee.

Robert Browning, "The Ring and the Book"

The Poetry Oracle

Why were you born when the snow was falling?

Christina Rossetti, "A Dirge"

If God invited you to a party and said,
   "Everyone in the ballroom tonight
   will be my special guest," how
   would you then treat them
   when you arrived?
Indeed, indeed!

Hafiz

You left North Haven, anchored in its rock,
afloat in mystic blue....And now- you've left
for good. You can't derange, or re-arrange,
your poems again, (But the Sparrows cab their sing.)
The words won't change again. Sad friend, you cannot
change.

Elizabeth Bishop, "North Haven"

ie while you're alive and
be absolutely dead.
Then do whatever you
want: it's all good.

Bunan

I think God might be a little prejudiced.
For once He asked me to join Him on a walk
   through this world, and we gazed into
   every heart on this earth, and I noticed
   He lingered a bit longer before any
   face that was weeping, and before
   any eyes that were laughing.
And sometimes when we passed a soul
   in worship God too would kneel
   down.
I have come to learn: God adores His
   creation.

St. Francis of Assisi

Courage was mine, and I had mystery;
Wisdom was mine, and I had mastery

Wilfred Owen, "Strange Meeting"

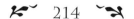

y peace is gone
My heart is sore
I'll find it never
Never more.

Johann Wolfgang von Goethe, "Faust"

If something my heart cherishes is
  taken away, I just say, "Lord,
  what happened?"
And a hundred more appear.

St. Catherine of Siena

And lives go on.
And lives go on
Like sudden lights
At street corners.

Donald Justice, "Bus Stop"

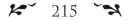 215

The Poetry Oracle

These hearts were woven of human joys and cares,
Washed marvellously with sorrow, swift to mirth.
The years had given them kindness. Dawn was theirs,
And sunset, and the colours of the earth.

Rupert Brooke, "The Dead"

Where he stands, the Arch Fear in a visible form,
    Yet the strong man must go.

Robert Browning, "Prospice"

The love of God, unutterable and perfect,
    flows into a pure soul the way that
    light rushes into a transparent object.

Dante

The Poetry Oracle

**If I should break the chain, I felt my bird would go;
Yet I must break the chain, or seal the prisoner's woe.**

Emily Bronte, "The Prisoner"

To learn the scriptures is easy, to live them, hard.
The search for the Real is no simple matter.
Deep in my looking, the last words vanished.
Joyous and silent, the waking that met me there.

Lalla

When the body becomes Your mirror,
   how can it serve?

Mahadeviyakka

The Poetry Oracle

Follow your saint, follow with accents sweet.
Thomas Campian

Heartless she is as the shadow in the meadows
　　Flying to the hills on a blue and breezy noon.

George Meredith, "Love in the Valley"

There's no room for lack of trust, or trust.
Nothing in this existence but that existence.
Rumi

The Poetry Oracle

How have you left the ancient love
That bards of old enjoy'd in you!

William Blake, "To the Muses"

Fade far away, dissolve, and quite forget
   What thou among the leaves has never known,
The weariness, the fever, and the fret
   Here, where men sit and hear each other groan.

John Keats, "Ode to a Nightingale"

Alleluia! light burst from your untouched
   womb like a flower on the farther side
   of death.
The world-tree is blossoming.
Two realms become one.

Hildegard of Bingen

Once my life is Your gesture, how can I pray?

Mahadeviyakka

If of herself she will not love,
    Nothing can make her:
    The devil take her!

Sir John Suckling, "Why So Pale and Wan?"

I give you my word
You pocket it
and keep the change.

Hettie Jones, "Words"

The Poetry Oracle

Who speaks the sound of an echo?
Who paints the image in a mirror?
Where are the spectacles in a dream?
Nowhere at all‐ that's the nature of mind!

Tree‐Leaf Woman

Amid all forms visible, the
spreading blades
I see as I move from place
to place.

Osage, "The Song of the Maize"

no

God dissolved my mind‐my separation.
I cannot describe now my intimacy with Him.
How dependent is your body's life on water
   and food and air?

Saint Theresa of Avila

The Poetry Oracle

8,000,000 alleluias

W.D. Snodgrass, "Snow Poems"

A little while alone in your room will prove
   more valuable than anything else that
   could ever be given you.

Rumi

The hale and maimed together
hurry to construct for the Buddha
a dwelling at each intersection.

Denise Levertov, "The Altars in the Street"

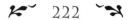

Rich the treasure;
    Sweet the pleasure;
Sweet is pleasure after pain.
John Dryden,
"Alexander's Feast Or, the Power of Music"

And when the slope feels gentle to the point
    that climbing up sheer rock is effortless
    as though you were gliding downstream
    in a boat, then you will have arrived
    where this path ends.

Dante

From the hag and hungry goblin
That into rags would rend ye,
    And the spirit that stands
    By the naked man
In the book of moons defend ye

Giles Earle, "Tom o' Bedlam's Song"

The Poetry Oracle

Fair fools delight to be accounted nice.
The richest corn dies if it be not reaped;
Beauty alone is lost, too warily kept.

Christopher Marlowe, "Hero and Leander"

Pause not to dream of the future before
      us;
Pause not to week the wild cares that
      come o'er us

Frances S. Osgood, "Labor"

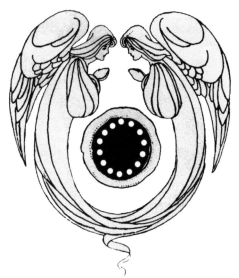

Change thy mind, since she doth change!
Let not fancy still abuse thee.

Robert Devereux, Earl of Essex, "Change thy Mind"

The Poetry Oracle

When all my awareness is Yours, what can there be to know?

Mahadeviyakka

you
can
rely
on
it

More of my days
I will not spend to gain an idiot's praise.

Thomas Randolph, "An ode to Mr. Anthony Stafford to hasten him into the country"

The sacred muse that first made love divine
Hath made him naked and without attire;
But I will clothe him with this pen of mine,
That all the world his fashion shall admire

Sir John Davies, "Gulling Sonnets"

The Poetry Oracle

Ah, why did Fate his steps decoy
    In stormy paths to roam,
Remote from all congenial joy?—
    O take the Wanderer home!

James Beattie, "Retirement: An Ode"

The sky and the strong wind have
    moved the spirit inside me till
    I am carried away trembling
    with joy.

Uvavnuk "Netsilik Eskimo"

Quiet yourself.
Reach out with your
mind's skillful hand.

St. John of the Cross

ind up the sagging breasts of morning
oh my darling let the light in.
Richard Shelton,
"The Fourteenth Anniversary"

For how long did I stand in the house of this
body and stare at the road?

Mira

We were kings!—Now around us fall the shadows
Of our serfdom like a raven's dropping wings.
Not a footstep of a fairy in the meadows—
Not a comrade who remembers we were kings!

Will H. Oglivie, "Kings in Exile"

"Sit down and have a drink" he says. I drink; we drink.
Frank O'Hara, "Why I Am Not A Painter"

Farewell, love, and all thy laws for ever,
Thy baited hooks shall tangle me no more.

Sir Thomas Wyatt, "A Renouncing of Love"

To see a World in a Grain of Sand
and a Heaven in a Wild Flower,
hold Infinity in the palm of your
Hand and Eternity in an hour.

William Blake, "Auguries of Innocence"

The Poetry Oracle

Ink runs from the corners of my mouth.
There is no happiness like mine.
I have been eating poetry.

Mark Strand, "Eating Poetry"

One star
   Is better far
      Than many precious stones.

Thomas Traherne, "The Apostarty"

The Truth has shared so much of
   Itself with me that I can no
   longer call myself a man,
   a woman, an angel, or
   even pure Soul.

Hafiz

229

The Poetry Oracle

I'll do as much for my true-love
  As any young man may;
I'll sit and mourn all at her grave
  For a twelvemonth and a day.

Anonymous, Traditional Ballad. "The Unquiet Grave"

I sing of apricot and brass. Hidden
coals glow sienna, almost out of sight.

Pamela Crow, "Here"

Om
Shanti Shanti Om
The Buddha

The Poetry Oracle

What I know best is a little thing.
It sits on the far side of the simile,
The like that's like the like.

Charles Wright, "California Dreaming"

When to the sessions of sweet silent thought
I summon up remembrance of things past,
I sigh the lack of many a thing I sought.

William Shakespeare, "Sonnet XXX"

Draw, draw the closed curtains: and make room:
My dear, my dearest dust; I come, I come.
Lady Catherine Dyer, "Epitaph on the Monument of Sir William Dyer at
Colmworth, 1641"

Flowers bloom.
Flowers die.
More is less.
I long for more.

Mark Strand, "The One Song"

I'd rather be a swineherd in the hut, understood
by swine, than be a poet misunderstood by men.

John Logan, "To a Young Poet Who Fled"

before the leaves have formed
you can glimpse the Christ and Thieves
on top of the hill. One of them was saved.
that day the snow had seemed to drop like grace.

John Logan, "Spring of the Thief"

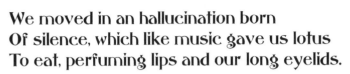

We moved in an hallucination born
Of silence, which like music gave us lotus
To eat, perfuming lips and our long eyelids.

Edith Sitwell, "Colonel Fantock"

I am severing all ties
With the parts of you
That swing from the rafters and
Hang from the trees

perine parker, "marked up"

At this hour I am always happy,
ready to be taken myself, fully aware.

Lucien Stryk, "Awakening"

he lived in grace and beauty
but never could she rid
herself the raven's
guilty whisper

Lizzy Lee Savage, "epitaph"

Move within, but don't move the way fear
makes you move.

Rumi

No, fear not your wild thoughts
It is your mind that will keep you safe

ArtAmiss, "fortune"

atience be all to thee.

Saint Theresa of Avila

"All wars are boyish," Herman Melville said;
But we are old, our fields are running wild:
Till Christ again turn wanderer and child.

Robert Lowell, "Christmas Eve Under Hooker's Statue"

Who will slap
    my backside
When I am born
    again.

Elise Cowen, "Who Will Slap…"

What is it you want to change? Your hair, your face,
  your body? Why? For God is in love
  with all those things and He might
  weep when they are gone.

St. Catherine of Siena

In the fire of its making, Gold doesn't vanish: The
  fire brightens.

Mechtild of Magdeburg

my path is pointed
conceived of reasons unknown

G. Thomas, "untitled"

The Poetry Oracle

If you circumambulated every holy shrine in the world
ten times, it would not get you to heaven as quick
as controlling your anger.

Kabir

I don't feel that I have clarified enough or
justified enough.

Jane Bowles, "Emmy Moore's Journal"

Bungee cords make perfect garters

Chromazona, "Sweet Cheeks"

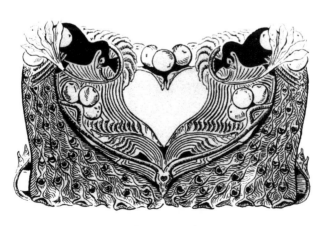

The Poetry Oracle

we swallow
and clink together
the last pieces of
our
tinkertoy brains

perine parker "downtown"

Don't you want to be the gracious host
In a lovely home of which you're proud to boast?
When my girl friends come to call
We've got to have carpeting from wall to wall.

Helen Adam, "Apartment On Twin Peaks"

Be the battle lost or won,
Though its smoke shall hide the sun,
I shall find my love—the one
Born for me!
Bret Harte, "What the Bullet sang"

your friends are the key

The poem
Is seen from all sides,
Everywhere,
At once.

Gary Snyder, "As For Poets"

There was just a continent without much on it
under a sky that never cared less.

William Stafford, "At The Bomb Testing Site"

I MUST not think of thee; and, tired yet strong,
I shun the love that lurks in all delight

Alice Meynell, "Renouncement"

nd tell those friends
About whom you forgot
That only half the word
Is merd and rot.

Madeline Gleason, "The Poet In The Wood"

His morning is not thine: yet must thou own
They have a cheerful warmth–those ashes on the stone

Thomas Edward Brown, "Salve!"

Gather a shell from the strewn beach,
And listen at its lips; they sigh
The same desire and mystery,
The echo of the whole sea's speech.

Dante Gabriel Rossetti, "The Sea-Limits"

The Poetry Oracle

Friendship's face he loveth well:
'Tis a countenance whose spell
Sheds a balm o'er every mead and dell
Where we used to fret.

Theodore Watts-Dunton, "Wassail Chorus at the Mermaid Tavern"

A box of counters and a red-vein'd stone,
A piece of glass abraded by the beach,
And six or seven shells,
A bottle with bluebells,
And two French copper coins, ranged there with careful art,
To comfort his sad heart.

Coventry Patmore, "The Toys"

I have left you behind
    In the path of the past,
With the white breath of flowers,
With the best of God's hours,
I have left you at last.

Dora Sigerson, "Ireland"

ontrarious moods of men
recoil away
  And isolate pure spirits,
and permit
  A place to stand and love
in for a day

Elizabeth Barrett Browning, "Sonnets from the Portuguese V"

For he saw what she did not see,
 That—as kindled by its own fervency—
The verge shrivell'd inward smoulderingly

Francis Thompson, "The Poppy"

Center of all centers, core of cores, almond
  self-enclosed and growing sweet – all
  this universe, to the furthest stars
  and beyond them, is your flesh,
  your fruit.

Rainer Maria Rilke

ternal substance I do see,
With which enriched I would be;
What is invisible to thee.

Anne Bradstreet, "The Flesh and the Spirit"

'YE have robb'd,' said he, 'ye have slaughter'd and
made an end,
   Take your ill-got plunder, and bury the dead:
What will ye more of your guest and sometime friend?'
'Blood for our blood,' they said.

Henry Newbolt, "He fell among Thieves"

When there is no place
  For the glow-worm to lie,
When there is no space
  For receipt of a fly;
When the midge dares not venture
Lest herself fast she lay,
If Love come, he will enter
  And will find out the way.

Anonymous, Seventeenth Century "Love will find out the Way"

The Poetry Oracle

The sodger frae the wars returns,
   The sailor frae the main;
But I hae parted frae my love,
   Never to meet again,
      My dear- Never to meet again.

Robert Burns, "The Farewell"

Life is but thought: so think I will
That Youth and I are housemates still.

Samuel Taylor Coleridge, "Youth and Age"

concentrate
and
ask
again

I drove down an aisle of sound,
nothing real but in the bell,
past the town where I was born

William Stafford, "Across Kansas"

The Poetry Oracle

Which way to heaven?
And where was love,
NEAR FAR NEVER
forgot your name.

Madeline Gleason,
"I Forgot Your Name"

Now air is hush'd, save where the weak-eyed bat
With short shrill shriek flits by on leathern wing

William Collins, "Ode to Evening"

There is no living wind astir;
　　The bat's unholy wing
Threads through the noiseless olive trees,
　　Like some unquiet thing
Which playeth in the darkness, when
　　The leaves are whispering.

Nathaniel Hawthorne, "The Star of Calvary"

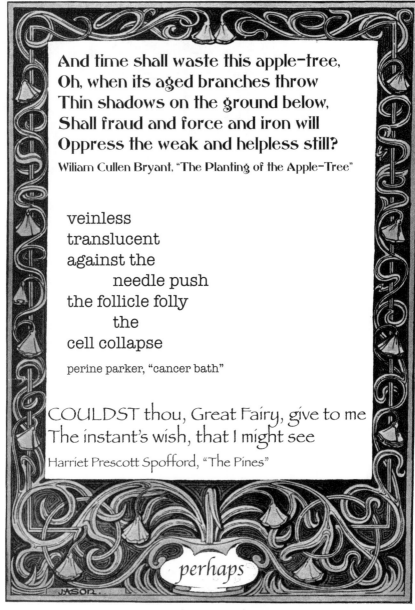

And time shall waste this apple-tree,
Oh, when its aged branches throw
Thin shadows on the ground below,
Shall fraud and force and iron will
Oppress the weak and helpless still?

Wiliam Cullen Bryant, "The Planting of the Apple-Tree"

> veinless
> translucent
> against the
>   needle push
> the follicle folly
>   the
> cell collapse

perine parker, "cancer bath"

COULDST thou, Great Fairy, give to me
The instant's wish, that I might see

Harriet Prescott Spofford, "The Pines"

perhaps

The Poetry Oracle

In a field
I am the absence
of field.
Mark Strand, "Keeping
Things Whole"

I've really had a mad year although now
perhaps I've come to a resting point...
Joan Burroughs, "Literary Outlaw"

And her proud, dark eyes wear a softened look
    As she watches the dying embers fall:
Perhaps she dream of the knight in the book,
Perhaps of the pictures that smile on the wall.

William Gordon McCabe, "Dreaming in the Trenches"

nwilling, alone we embark,
And the things we have seen
and have known and have
heard of, fail us.

Robert Bridges, "On a Dead Child"

And each victor, passing wanly,
Gazes on that Presence lonely,
With unmoving eyes where only
Grow the dreams for which men die.

Madison Julius Cawein, "Attainment"

Of all things beautiful and good,
The kingliest is brotherhood.

Edwin Markham, "Brotherhood"

he too accepts the truth,
there is no way back.

Denise Levertov, "Stele (i–IIc. B.C.)"

These things in which we have seen ourselves and spoken?
Ask us, prophet, how we shall call
Our natures forth when that live tongue is all
Dispelled, that glass obscured or broken.

Richard Wilbur, "Advice To A Prophet"

O, well for him that knows and early know
In his own soul the rose
Secretly burgeons, of this earthly flower
The heavenly paramour.

Alfred Noyes, "The Two Worlds"

When brother shall with brother walk in peace,
Watching the kindly fruits of earth increase;
And all the energies beneath the dome
Shall find the harmony that roots in Home

Richard Burton, "The Plan"

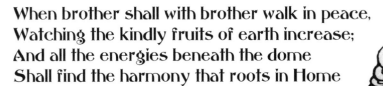

I know that no flower, no flint was in vain
on the path I trod.

Amelia Josephine Burr, "A Song of Living"

I would make a list against the evil days
      Of lovely things to hold in memory
Richard Le Gallienne, "A Ballade-Catalogue of Lovely Things"

The Poetry Oracle

What riches have you that deem me poor,
Or what large comfort that you call me sad?

George Santayana, "What Riches Have You"

He didn't know much music
        When first he come along;
An' al the birds went wonderin'
        Why he didn't sing a song?

Frank Lebby Stanton, "The Mocking-Bird"

O you that still have rain and sun,
Kisses of children and of wife,
And the good earth to tread upon,
And the mere sweetness of life,
Forget not us, who gave all these
For something dearer, and for you.

Laurence Binyon, "From the Dead to the Living"

LOVE thy country, wish it well,
Not with too intense a care;
'Tis enough that, when it fell,
Thou its ruin didst not share

George Bubb Dodington, Lord Melcombe,

"Shorten Sail"

Be as I content
With my old lament
And my idle dream.

Robert Bridges, "Clear and Gentle Stream"

Lord, in this hour of tumult,
    Lord, in this night of fears,
Keep open, oh, keep open
    My eyes, my ears.

Hermann Hagedorn, "Prayer During Battle"

ow rain, now sun, now clouds
that jackknife in between.

Rod McKuen, "Hand in Hand"

a bee buzzed through
my open window
following the breeze
and the quiet order of things.

Jolene G., "Chaos"

Oh, what is so good as the urge of it,
And what is so glad as the surge of it,
And what is so strong as the summons deep,
Rousing the torpid soul from sleep?

Angela Morgan, "Work"

**Comrades, pour the wine tonight
For parting is with dawn!**

Richard Hovey, "Comrades"

Yet no blind fears distress the thoughtful soul.

David Fallon, "Nature's Miracle"

Faithful paranoid
It's all One to you
　　　isn't it
Real, that is.

Elise Cowen, "Death"

The Poetry Oracle

It is good to be out on the road, and going one knows not
Where.

John Masefield, "Teweksbury Road"

He whom a dream hath possessed treads the implacable
Marches.

Shaemas O'Sheel, "He Whom a Dream Hath Possessed"

God mend thine every flaw,
Confirm thy soul in self-control,
Thy liberty thy law!

Katharine Lee Bates, "America the Beautiful"

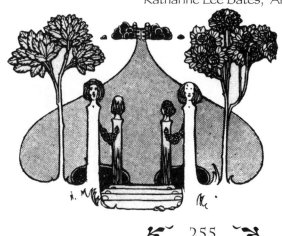

The Poetry Oracle

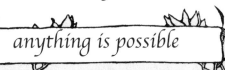

anything is possible

It matters not how strait the gate,
  How charged with punish-
ments the scroll,
I am the master of my fate:
  I am the captain of my soul.

William Ernest Henley, "Invictus"

You come upon it suddenly—you
cannot seek it out:
It's like a secret still unheard and
never noised about.

Charles Hannon Towne, "The Best Road of All"

folklore extremis is a
  deadly disease only
cured by offering water

Brenda Knight, "speed poem, part 1"

choose to live life

The river that flows
Over the rock
Hesitates
At the dam

Dolores G., "A Higher-ku"

I will laugh with the wicked
I will cry with the heathens
and I will dance for my dead.

Bucky Sinister, "Shine"

Let me live in a house by the side of the road
 Where the race of men go by—
The men who are good and the men who are bad,
 As good and bad as I.

Sam Walter Foss, "The House by the Side of the Road"

Reader, by now you must be sure
you know just where we are,
deep in symbolic woods.
Irony, self-accusation,
someone else's suffering.
The search is that of art.

William Matthews, "The Search Party"

I know they boast they souls to souls convey:
Howe'er they meet, the body is the way.

William Cartwright, "No Platonique Love"

Meditate within eternity. Don't stay in the mind.
Your thoughts are like a child fretting near
   its mother's breast, restless and
   afraid, who with a little guidance,
   can find the path of courage.

Lalla

hall I go bound and you go free,
And love one so removed from me?

Padraic Colum, "Shall I Go Bound and You Go Free?"

Still through the cloven skies they come,
With peaceful wings unfurled;
And still their heavenly music floats
O'er all the weary world

Edmund Hamilton Sears, "The Angels' Song"

From too much love of living,
From hope and fear set free,
We thank with brief thanksgiving
Whatever gods may be.

Algernon Charles Swinburne, "The Garden of Proserpine"

The Poetry Oracle

Are you jealous of the ocean's generosity?
Why would you refuse to give this joy
   to anyone?
Fish don't hold the sacred liquid in cups.
They swim the huge fluid freedom.

Rumi

All that we see or seem
Is but a truth within a dream.

Edgar Allan Poe, "A Dream Within a Dream"

Life is given.
Nothing is earned, so learn to serve others,
   not your own desire and greed
   and ego.
They steel your energies, whereas devotion
   builds your strength and protects the
   intelligent flame that leads to the
   truth within.

Lalla

The Poetry Oracle

I walk slow through day break-blue. back to north beach.
my lids fold around my whole being.

ruth weiss, "I Always Thought You Black"

O where are you going? stay with me here!
     Were the vows you swore me deceiving?
No, I promised to love you, dear,
     But I must be leaving.

W.H. Auden, "O What Is that Sound"

If you want money more than anything, you'll be
  bought and sold.
If you have a greed for food, you'll be
  a loaf of bread.
This is a subtle truth:
  whatever you love, you are.

Rumi

The Poetry Oracle

He who, from zone to zone,
Guides through the boundless sky thy certain flight,
In the long way that I must tread alone,
　　Will lead my steps aright.

William Cullen Bryant, "To a Waterfowl"

There is no snow in Hollywood
there is no rain in California
I have been to lots of parties
and acted perfectly disgraceful
but I never actually collapsed.

Frank O'Hara, "Poem"

He who replies with words of Doubt
Doth put the light of knowledge out.

William Blake, "Auguries of Innocence"

The Poetry Oracle

In the heats of hate and lust
    In the house of flesh are strong,
Let me mind the house of dust
    Where my sojourn shall be long.

A.E. Houseman, "From a Shropshire Lad"

How funny you are today New York
like Ginger Rogers in Swingtime.

Frank O'Hara, "Steps"

Since moons decay and suns decline
How else should I end this life of mine?

John Masefield, "The Passing Strange"

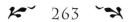

The Poetry Oracle

Did I go mad in my mother's womb

**Waiting
to get out.**

Elise Cowen, "Did I Go Mad"

Are you jealous of the ocean's generosity?
Why would you refuse to give this joy
   to anyone?
Fish don't hold the sacred liquid in cups.
They swim the huge fluid freedom.

Rumi

Her pleasure will not let me stay.
She talks and I am fain to list.

Robert Lee Frost, "My November Guest"

The Poetry Oracle

They're cheering from the ferries,
    And they're waving from the shore;
The dull old life's behind us
    And the new life lies before.

Anonymous, "Sailing Orders"

When will my shame fall away?
When will I accept being mocked
   and let my robe of dignity burn up?

Lalla

Don't get old and mean and bitter, —there's a
      Primal remedy—
Just take a ship to sea, my lad, just take a ship to sea.

Harry Kemp, "The Remedy"

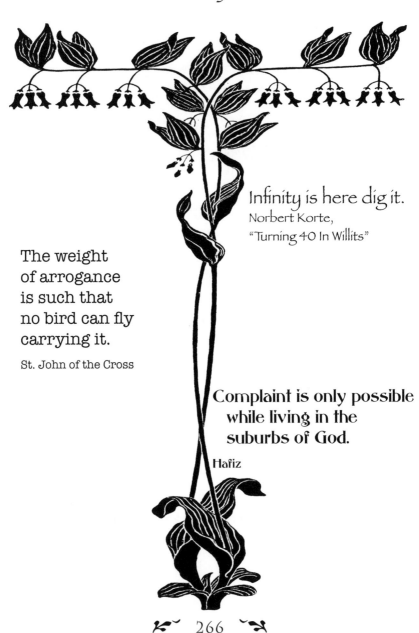

Infinity is here dig it.
Norbert Korte,
"Turning 40 In Willits"

The weight
of arrogance
is such that
no bird can fly
carrying it.

St. John of the Cross

Complaint is only possible
while living in the
suburbs of God.

Hafiz

The Poetry Oracle

We shall remember, when our hair is white,
These clouded days revealed in radiant light.

George Orwell, "Our Minds Are Married, But We Are Too Young"

I do not doubt I am limitless, and that the universes
are limitless-- in vain I try to think how limitless

Walt Whitman, "Assurances"

It is your destiny to see as God sees,
    to know as God knows,
    to feel as God feels.

Meister Eckhart, "Germany"

I had a natural passion for fine clothes, excellent food, and
   lively conversation about all matters that concern
   the heart still alive. And even a passion
   about my own
   looks.
Vanities: they do not exist.

Saint Theresa of Avila, "Spain"

And henceforth I will go celebrate anything I see or am,
And sing and laugh, and deny nothing.

Walt Whitman, "All is Truth"

Lay down these words
Before your mind like rocks.
        placed solid, by hands.

Gary Snyder, "Riprap"

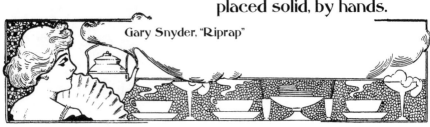

The Poetry Oracle

I have had to learn the simplest things
last. Which made for difficulties,
Even at sea I was slow, to get the hand out, or to cross
A wet deck.
The sea was not, finally, my trade.

Charles Olson, "Maximus, To Himself"

It's the old shell trick with a twist:
I saw God put Himself in one
    of your pockets.
You are bound
    to find Him.

Tukaram

I wish for such a lot of things
That never will come true,
And yet I want them all so much
I think they might, don't you?

Sara Teasdale, "Wishes"

269

The Poetry Oracle

It is always a matter, my darling,
Of life or death, as I had forgotten. I wish
What I wished you before, but harder.

Richard Wilbur, "The Writer"

**My friend at last comes back. Maybe the right words
were there all along.**
Complicity. Wonder.

C.K. Williams, "The Gas Station"

He openly declared that it was the best sign
Of good store of wit to have good store of coin.

Sir John Suckling, "A session of the poets"

The Poetry Oracle

More time, more time. Barrages of applause
Come muffled from a buried radio.
The New-year bells are wrangling with the snow.

Richard Wilbur, "Year's End"

O well for him whose will is strong!
He suffers, but he will not suffer long;
He suffers, but he cannot suffer wrong.

Alfred Lord Tennyson, "Will"

The thing you're after
May lie around the bend.

Charles Olson, "I, Maximus of Gloucester, To You"

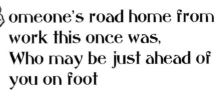

omeone's road home from work this once was,
Who may be just ahead of you on foot

Robert Frost, "Directive"

I cannot dance, O Lord, unless You lead me.

Mechtild of Magdeburg

O how feeble is man's power,
    That if good fortune fall,
Cannot add another hour
    Nor a lost hour recall.

John Donne, "Song"

Love in her eyes sits playing,
        And sheds delicious death.

John Gay, "Love in Her Eyes Sits Playing"

What I most want
    is to spring out of this personality,
    then to sit apart from that leaping.
I've lived too long where I can be reached.

Rumi

If sadly thinking
With spirits sinking,
Could more than drinking
        My cares compose.

John Philpot Curran, "The Deserter"

Give all to love;
Obey thy heart

Ralph Waldo Emerson, "Give All to Love"

He wrote with no apparent hesitation, quickly,
and with concentration;
    his inspiration was inspiring.

C.K. Williams, "The Critic"

Love is form, and cannot be without
important substance (the weight
say, 58 carats each one of us, perforce
our goldsmith's scale).

Charles Olson, "I, Maximus of Gloucester, To You"

The Poetry Oracle

God is a pure no-thing, concealed in now and here:
   the less you reach for him, the more
   he will appear.

Angelus Silesius

Say not the struggle nought availeth,
      The labour and the wounds are vain,
The enemy faints not, nor faileth,
      And as things have been things remain.

Arthur Hugh Clough, "Say not the struggle nought availeth"

Some day the viewless latch will lift,
      The door of air swing wide.

Henry Augustin Beers, "Ecce in Deserto"

Love, you have wrecked my body. Keep doing that.
I am more well with this deep ache of missing
  you than content with the physical wonders
  you can pacify us with.

Mira

Three silences there are: the first of speech,
The second of desire, the third of thought

John Greenleaf Whittier, "The Three Silences of Molinos"

ask
again
later

I wonder when the tide will flow
Sir Oracle cease saying, "No"

John Davidson, "Rondeau"

Pretentious
giving me
what in the instant
I knew better of.

Charles Olson,
"The Librarian"

Dear God, please reveal to us your sublime
beauty that is everywhere, everywhere,
everywhere, so that we will never again
feel frightened.
My divine love, my love, please let us touch
your face.

St. Francis of Assisi

Build as though wilt, unspoiled by praise or blame,
Build as thou wilt, and as thy light is given.

Thomas Bailey Aldrich, "Enamored Architect of Airy Rhyme"

I ask all blessings, I ask them with reverence,
  of my mother earth, of the sky, moon,
  and sun my father.
I am old age: the essence of life, I am the
  source of all happiness.
All is peaceful, all in beauty, all in harmony,
  all in joy.

Anonymous. "Navajo"

Order is a lovely thing;
On disarray it lays its wing,
Teaching simplicity to sing.

Anna Hempstead Branch, "The Monk in the Kitchen"

I drag a boat over the ocean with a solid rope.
Will God hear? Will he take me all the way?

Lalla

The Poetry Oracle

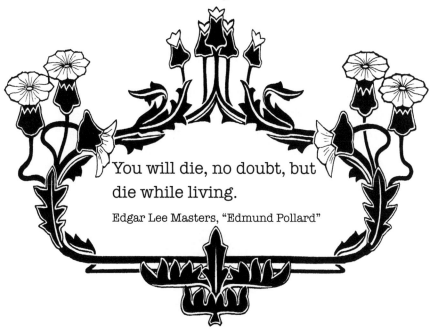

You will die, no doubt, but die while living.

Edgar Lee Masters, "Edmund Pollard"

God was an accident of language, a quirk
of the unconscious mind, but
Unhappily never of my mind.

C.K. Williams, "The Ladder"

The Mind severe and cool;
The Heart still half a fool;
The fine-spun Soul, a beam of sun can startle.

Elinor Wylie, "This Corruptible"

The Poetry Oracle

Tread near the living, consecrated thing,
Treasure me thy cast youth.

Francis Thompson, "Before her Portrait in Youth"

the
reply
is yes

With your bucket of water, and mop, and
    Brush,
Bringing her out of the grime.

Thomas Hardy, "The Statue of Liberty"

These two have striven half the day,
    And each prefers his separate claim,—
    Poor rivals in a losing game,
That will not yield each other way.

Alfred Lord Tennyson, "In Memoriam A. H. H."

The Poetry Oracle

You tell too many lies and hurt your-
self:
You don't like what you only like too
much.

Robert Browning, "Fra Lippo Lippi"

What canst thou say or do of charm
enough
To dull the nice remembrance of my
home?

John Keats, "Lamia"

Leave the sick hearts
that honor could
not move

Rupert Brooke, "Peace"

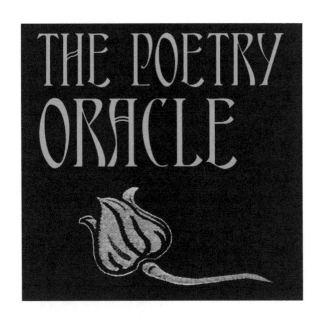

Dedicated to the loving memory of
Robert Kent Leffler

Acknowledgments

To all the billies, the beats, the seers, the saints
The poets, the pagans, and the pirates
To our ever-loving and deadline-forgiving publisher and
friend Brad Olsen
To the Leos, the Steampunks, the stars
To the Pisces husband and the lifelong lovers and friends
Elizabeth Jens and the ladies of Troupe de Trash
We thank you
You know who you are
And you know how to find us
Write us a speed poem about it.

The Poetry Oracle

Bibliography

Aldington, Richard. The Viking Book of Poetry of the English Speaking World, Vol. 1.**Viking Press: 1958, New York.**

Alvarez, Alicia. Bedtime: 365 Nightly Readings for Passion and Romance. **Conari Press: 1995, Berkeley.**

Astrov, Margot. American Indian Prose and Poetry. **Capricorn Books: 1962, New York**

Benet, William and Conrad Aiken. An Anthology of Famous English and American Poetry. **The Modern Library/Random House: 1945, New York.**

Bloom, Harold. The Best Poems of the English Language. **Harper Collins: 2004. New York, New York.**

Brown, E.K. Victorian Poetry. **Thomas Nelson and Sons: 1942, New York.**

Burr, David Stanford. Love Poems. **Barnes & Noble: 2002, New York, New York.**

Cooper, Alice Cecilia. Poems of Today. **Ginn and Company: 1924, Boston.**

The Poetry Oracle

Dickinson, Emily. Selected Poems. **Dover: 1990, New York.**

Douglas, George. The Book of Scottish Poetry. **T. Fisher Unwin: 1911, London.**

Eliot, G.R. and Norman Foerster. English Poetry of the Nineteenth Century. **Macmillan: 1935, New York.**

Fowler, Alastair. The New Oxford Book of Seventeenth Century Verse. **Oxford University Press: 1992, Oxford/ New York.**

Frothingham, Robert. Songs of the Sea & Sailors' Chanteys. **Houghton Mifflin: 1924, Cambridge, MA.**

Goodwin, Daisy. 101 Poems That Could Save Your Life. **Harper Collins: 2003, New York, New York.**

Harmon, William. The Top 500 Poems. **Columbia University Press: 1992, New York, New York.**

Hebel, J. William and Hoyt H. Hudson. Poetry of the English Renaissance 1509-1660. **Appleton-Century Crofts: 1929, New York.**

Hyde, Douglas. Love Songs of Connacht. **Barnes & Noble: 1969, New York.**

Kaufman, Alan. The Outlaw Bible of American Poetry. **Thunder's Mouth Press: 1999, New York.**

The Poetry Oracle

Keats, John. Lyric Poems. Dover: 1991,New York,.

Lattimore, Richmond. Greek Lyrics. The University of Chicago Press: 1960, Chicago.

Martz, Louis Lohr, Ed. Anchor Anthology of Seventeenth-Century Verse Volume 1, (and 2) Anchor Books: 1969, Garden City, New York

McKuen, Rod. Hand in Hand. Pocket Books: 1977. New York, NY

Nicholson, D.H.S. and Lee A.H.E. The Oxford Book of English Mystical Verse. Clarendon Press, Oxford: 1917

Plath, Sylvia. Ariel: The Restored Edition. Harper Collins: 2004, New York.

Quiller-Couch, Arthur Thomas, Sir. The Oxford Book of Ballads. Clarendon Press, Oxford: 1910.

Quiller-Couch, Arthur Thomas, Sir. The Oxford Book of English Verse. Clarendon Press: Oxford, 1901.

Rittenhouse, Jessie Belle. The Little Book of Modern Verse. Houghton Miffflin: Boston, 1917.

Rossetti, Christina. Goblin Market and Other Poems. Dover: 1994, New York.

Sewell, Marilyn. Claiming the Spirit Within. Beacon Press: 1996, Boston.

The Poetry Oracle

Shakespeare, William. Measure for Measure. **New American Library: 1964, New York**

Sinister, Bucky. All Blacked Out and Nowhere to Go. **Gorsky Press: 2007, Los Angeles.**

Smith, Phillip, Ed. 100 Best-Loved Poems. **Dover Books: 1995, Mineola, New York.**

Tedlock, Dennis. Finding the Center: Narrative Poetry of the Zuni Indians. **The Dial Press: 1972. New York**

Whicher, George F. The Goliard Poets. **Cambridge University Press: 1944, Cambridge, MA.**

Zeydel, Edwin. Vagabond Verse. **Wayne State University Press: 1966, Detroit.**

The following link proved tremendously useful for finding sources for poetry:

www.bartleby.com

goodbye

Other Books by CCC Publishing:

KEY TO SOLOMON'S KEY
SECRETS OF MAGIC AND MASONRY

"DuQuette's book carries a ticking religious time-bomb of historic proportions just waiting to explode. The implications for our times are provocative." —*Arthur Rosengarten*

ISBN 1888729147   208 pages $14.95 by: Lon Milo DuQuette

SACRED PLACES OF GODDESS: 108 DESTINATIONS

"'Provides background information on a site's ancient or new importance. Some sections have warnings about deterioration at some sites; these are called 'Gai Alerts,' after the Greek goddess personifying Earth." —*Los Angeles Times*

ISBN: 1888729112   424 pages $19.95   by: Karen Tate

SACRED PLACES NORTH AMERICA 2ND EDITION

"*Sacred Places North America* is a revealing, useful, and enthusiastically recommended guide." —*Midwest Book Review*

ISBN 1888729139   408 pages $19.95   by: Brad Olsen

SACRED PLACES AROUND THE WORLD 2ND EDITIO

"(Readers) will thrill to the wonderful history and the vibration of the world's sacred healing places." —*East & West*

ISBN 1888729104   288 pages $17.95   by: Brad Olsen

SACRED PLACES EUROPE: 108 DESTINATIONS

"Explores the rich cultural, spiritual landscape through all points of the compass." —*Nexus*

ISBN: 1888729120   344 pages $19.95   by: Brad Olsen

All Consortium of Collective Consciousness Publishing books are distribute by: Independent Publishers Group: (800) 888-4741   www.ipgbook.com

FOR INDIVIDUAL ORDERS AND MORE: www.cccpublishing.com